STUDENT
SUCCESS

How to be *Original*

Transform Your Assignments and Achieve Better Grades

Alastair Bonnett

S Sage

1 Oliver's Yard
55 City Road
London EC1Y 1SP

2455 Teller Road
Thousand Oaks
California 91320

Unit No 323-333, Third Floor, F-Block
International Trade Tower
Nehru Place, New Delhi – 110 019

8 Marina View Suite 43-053
Asia Square Tower 1
Singapore 018960

Editor: Kate Keers
Associate editor: Sahar Jamfar
Production editor: Imogen Roome
Copyeditor: Sarah Bury
Proofreader: Leigh Smithson
Marketing manager: Catherine Slinn
Cover design: Sheila Tong
Typeset by: C&M Digitals (P) Ltd, Chennai, India
Printed in the UK

Library of Congress Control Number: 2022951117

British Library Cataloguing in Publication data

A catalogue record for this book is available from the British Library

ISBN 978-1-5296-2184-6
ISBN 978-1-5296-2183-9 (pbk)

How to be

Original

Get the skills you need to succeed!

Student Success books are essential guides for students of all levels. From how to think critically and write great essays to planning your dream career, the Student Success series helps you study smarter and get the best from your time at university.

Test yourself with practical tasks

YOUR PROGRESS

Diagnose your strengths and weaknesses

min   max

Dial up your skills for improved grades

Visit **sagepub.co.uk/study-skills**
for free tips and resources for study success

Contents

CONTENTS

Author biography

Alastair Bonnett is Professor of Geography at Newcastle University. His books have been translated into nineteen languages and include *The Age of Islands: In Search of New and Disappearing Islands* and *Multiracism: Rethinking Racism in Global Context.*

Acknowledgements

Thanks to Kate Keers, Sahar Jamfar, Sarah Bury, Imogen Roome, Helen Caunce and Rachel Holland for their helpful advice and editorial skills.

Introduction

Anyone can be original.

And originality is the key. It opens doors to excellent grades and success. It's a stated criterion for top marks. Yet it is not taught or even explained. Originality is one of the last redoubts of mysticism: students are marked down for not providing it but no one tells them what it is. Originality is widely considered innate; ineffable; hard to explain. It isn't. With a little guidance anyone can be original.

There is no mystery to originality. I first realised this 40 years ago. I was a first-year student and I had to deliver a talk on nationalism for one of my seminars. I was terrified, fear constricted my throat and I gabbled through the few minutes allotted to my presentation. Those able to hear any of it would have found out that I'd chosen to focus on nationalism in small island states. My talk was bad, that much was clear, so I was baffled when I got a half-decent mark. 'Very original' came the feedback. All I had done was give the set topic an unexpected context.

Something had worked. My modest shift of context had somehow sprinkled stardust onto a rubbish heap. It was my first lesson in the fact that originality is very far from the stuff of magic: it can be simple and it is learnable. There are straightforward techniques that you can master that will transform your work and make it stand out.

Before we can make use of any of them, we need to understand why and how being original can help you. Let's start by looking at the assessment criteria that college staff often gesture to but which, when you read them, are nearly always exercises in the obvious. I have a bunch in front of me from different universities. I read in this one that the highest marks are awarded to work that has 'insight' and is 'excellent'. Another explains that lower grades are given to material that show a 'weak grasp of concepts'. And so it goes on. No wonder so few students read these benchmarks . But one word jumps out, lurking in the highest bands, where 'outstanding' marks are given. That word is 'original'. Makes an 'original contribution', 'shows originality', 'evidence of originality' – in almost every example I have before me it's there; it is the key term in explaining why top marks are handed out.

Originality is set up on a golden throne: it is 'exceptional', the scholarly grail. The unmissable implication is that it is for the few, not the many; the top 1 per cent. But this is nonsense. It's no such thing. Anyone can be original.

Here's an example. Imagine you have been assigned an essay on government support for the arts. The lecture and the reading list both contain a lot of information on public support for museums and art galleries. But you notice that one of the authors also writes about government support for arts education among children. It's a slender thread but it's worth pulling. At the start of your essay, you lean on this author – *work with* their ideas – to explain why support for children's arts in museums and galleries is going to be your focus. It's not a huge thing: you haven't reinvented the wheel. No genius required. But, amid the dozens, hundreds even, of other submissions all about general policies concerning museums and art galleries that your assessor will soon be weighed down with, your essay will appear rare and thoughtful.

We have already learned three things about originality: (a) *it's not beyond you*; (b) a *shift in context* can be enough; (c) *keep it simple*. If you do one original thing it's going to have more impact than a cluster of novelties.

Perhaps we have also learnt a fourth. Even though originality is within your grasp, that's not the same thing as saying originality is quick and easy. If you're not prepared to do the work, then it is better to play safe. Originality is rarely a rush job. In Chapter 1 I walk you through the preparation that is required. You need to give yourself time to try out different options, some of which may not work out, and you'll also probably need more time again to do a bit of reading that is beyond the set list.

Why? Originality needs justification

The single biggest obstacle you face is a one-word question: 'Why?' Originality only counts if it is a useful thing to do; if it advances our understanding of an issue and contributes to a debate. The value of originality is not intrinsic or self-evident.

It is useful in the first or second paragraph of an assignment to have a sentence or two that directly tackles the 'why?' question. We can understand this better by looking at another example. Let's take the same scenario: you have been assigned an essay on government support for the arts. But this time your originality, your 'added value', is geographical. You are going to relocate the topic to Morocco. But why? What's the point of doing that? There are nearly 200 countries in the world: just harpooning a new one with no explanation looks arbitrary. Morocco is a large, well-known country so, perhaps, you might think its importance is self-evident. You would be wrong. *There is no such thing as self-evident.* You *have* to answer 'why?'. In this case it might be useful to write, for example, any or all of the following:

(a) In recent years Pink, Silver and other scholars (Green; Blue) have called for the internationalisation of the study of arts policy.
(b) Significant comparative insights into arts policies in other North African and Arab countries can be gained by looking at Morocco.
(c) The Moroccan government has instituted a distinct and influential approach to arts policy funding.

Here are three claims that explain 'why?'. The first one (a) tells us it matters because it follows a new direction in the literature; the second (b) explains that it matters because it opens up a wider field of study; and the third (c) suggests it matters because there is something instructive and special about this particular case. In academic work, the first of these is especially useful and can often suffice to answer 'why?'. After all, your work is, above all, an *engagement* with the literature. If you are able to say it responds, in some way, to an expert call to do the very thing you are doing, then 'why?' is reasonably well nailed. But a second nail is often handy and, in the sentence (a), the call for 'internationalisation' does not tell us 'why Morocco?'. So, in this case, you could usefully tack in a further explanation, such as (b) and/or (c).

For most assignments, having one or two (three if really needed) reasons 'why?' is enough. More than that can look like pleading. These reasons need to be pithy. In essays and exams where space is limited, they can be conveyed in a sentence or two. It can be helpful to return to them, especially in your conclusion.

TIP

The problem with the 'gap argument'

A gap argument states that something needs to be done because it hasn't been done. In the examples above, this would lead us to claim that there is little or no work on arts policy in Morocco, *therefore* there needs to be some. It sounds reasonable but it is not compelling. The problem is that gap arguments postpone the 'why?' question rather than answering it. *Why* fill this gap? It is not self-evident. The gap argument is not necessarily wrong – it can be part of an explanation – but it is never sufficient.

Your allies

Originality is exciting. It's bold. And when doing anything daring it is a good idea to have friends. Rooting your new idea in the work of an authority figure (often, the author of an academic paper or book) anchors it. This author (or authors – there can be more than one) is your ally. They provide you with validation, direction and justification.

Your allies may point the way in general terms. We saw this in the sentence (a) above which claimed that 'in recent years' some scholars 'have called for' the approach you are taking. Your allies may also give a more specific endorsement of your efforts, in effect by precursing your work. In either case, it is useful to explain that you are 'developing', 'drawing on', 'expanding' or, perhaps, 'critiquing' their work, and thus *contributing* to an original direction. Originality is always more than imitation. Rather, it tells us (1) that you acknowledge prior work; (2) that this prior work shows that the path you are taking is worthwhile; and (3) that you, in some way, are going to develop, divert or simply go further along this new road.

This may sound rather modest: you are *engaging* something that exists already. It's an ironic truth, but when it comes to academic originality, honesty and modesty are powerful. The most plausible and convincing forms of originality – and the ones likely to impress your assessors – are rarely self-aggrandising. Acknowledging previous work makes your work compelling.

Another ally worth thinking about is your audience. For students, your key audience is the person grading your work. If you want to do something original, then it can be helpful to get some feedback from that person before you submit your work. Sometimes this is straightforward: the course leader is the person marking the work and you feel able to consult them. Other times things are not so simple. Marking may be done by teaching assistants, of which there may be any number, and it may be sent off to places unknown to you. Usually there are still channels you can use to check whether your idea is going to be well received. But not always. Originality can be a lonely place. Don't give up. It is especially important in such circumstances to anchor the original aspects of your work in the literature and to make it clear that you are doing exactly what your assignment requires of you. Even if you have no contact with them, your assessors are human beings, and well-explained and anchored originality will be recognised and appreciated. For further discussion on where you can get help, see the section on 'Being part of a community of learners' in Chapter 1.

TIP

Show, don't tell

Phrases like 'I am being original because…' or 'this essay is original because …' should be avoided. They are clumsy, unnecessary, and are hostages to fortune. If you are explicit about how and why you are engaging and pushing forward a debate or topic then that is enough. Original thinkers do not rush around telling people how original they are: show, don't tell.

How to use this book

Chapter 1 introduces the preparatory work that is needed if you want to be original. Preparation is not an act of sitting back and pondering the sky, but of reading and critical engagement. To make full use of the three stages of preparation I introduce, you will need to have some ideas about the approach you want to take. You can get these by reading, or skimming, any or all of the book's other chapters.

Chapter 2 charts six straightforward techniques that can provide an original context for your work (we have already met a couple of them). For many students, this chapter will be the most important and some may decide to bolt through the rest of the book. That's fine: this isn't a novel but a toolbox. Any combination of Chapter 1 and any of the other five chapters will produce results.

Chapters 3 to 6 are more specific in intent but, depending on the task you have before you, any of them might be your key chapter. Chapter 3 is about how you communicate originality. Coming up with a pithy and effective phrase helps people understand what is different about your approach. As we shall see, 'new words' and innovative language open up a range of fascinating possibilities that can take your scholarship to a new level.

Originality is not just about your findings or argument. How you *do* research, the methods you use, can also be original. In Chapter 4 I explore methodological originality. There are many pioneering ways of collecting evidence, of *doing* research, and this is an area that can really make a difference in how your work is received. Chapter 5 is on originality and creativity and its focus is on how students in both the 'creative disciplines' (art, music, fashion or performance) and so-called 'non-creative disciplines' (which is everyone else) can be pioneering in 'arts-based practice'.

Chapter 6 is about originality in presentations and group work and through impact and dissemination. The latter two topics are points of near obsession within many higher education institutions and students can benefit from understanding and contributing to this effort. Presentations and group work are also sites where innovation can be well received, but, as we shall see, this is not the same thing as giving the green light to the wacky or eccentric. Effective originality, the innovations that impress, nearly always concern matters of intellectual substance.

I have titled the book's final instalment 'Staying Original' because the skills I'm going to introduce can serve you well into the future. Understanding that you too can be a pioneer, that it is within your grasp, is powerful knowledge. I also take the opportunity to reflect on the value of originality in a society in which every advert, every newsstand, proclaims the value of the new. This book does not argue that originality has intrinsic value, that it is always and everywhere a good thing. If it is not substantive, if it is not useful, then novelty is unwanted and unwarranted. *How to Be Original* is not designed to 'big up' originality but to demystify it; to show that it does not arise from alchemy, or the planet-sized brains of the very few, but from work and reading. There is no mystery and no magic to originality.

Note on my use of quotes and references

In order to craft useful sample sentences and case studies I have used both real quotes and references and invented ones. The invented ones are mostly found in the Introduction and in Chapters 2 and 3 and, more occasionally, in other chapters. It is easy to tell the difference. For the real quotes and references the full names of authors are given and the cited work can be found in the notes. The made-up authors are designated by a colour, for example 'Blue argues ...', 'Green explains ...'.

1

Preparations

Introduction

Anyone can be original but that doesn't mean it's as easy as tripping over a wet log.

This chapter explains the initial stages of originality. It depicts a process of closing in, starting with reading and exploring and ending up with something that is focused and structured. I'll explain three preparatory stages: reading and generating ideas; focusing and anchoring; and planning. I then turn to the way originality can be adapted for different assessments and levels. The difference in what is expected of a first-year exam and an 80,000-word PhD is vast. Originality is required in the latter but widely imagined to be beyond the capabilities of new students. It isn't. Students at all stages can produce innovative work. In the last part of the chapter, I address a subject that worries a lot of students, the politics of originality.

The three stages

1. Reading and generating ideas

Idea generation is not an exact science. You probably won't hit on exactly the right idea straight away. It is important not to expect to do so. This initial period is more akin to a fertile muddle than clockwork perfection. What you are aiming for in Stage 1 is to have one or, more likely, a small number (three or four) of ideas that promise to fulfil your assignment brief while being innovative. You can then go ahead to Stage 2 (focusing and anchoring). You will have doubts about some or even all of them, but that's OK. Doubt is good – it's not an enemy but a friend; you can accommodate it, adapting and refining your work, or use it to select another path.

Start with targeted browsing. More specifically, combine a word search based on the key terms in your assignment with one or more of the approaches outlined in Chapters 2 to 5.

Let's break this process down. First, type in the key term from your assignment title, or a closely related idea you are hoping to work with, into an academic search engine. Using the results, write down a short list of the approaches to the topic that appear intriguing. From this process you may arrive at a single chosen topic or several topics (up to four). Second, with the help of one or more of the examples found Chapters 2 to 5, note down the original approach you want to take. Summarise the result of the combination of these two steps in a sentence or two.

You do not need to read all the chapters of *How to Be Original* before you get started on this exercise. You can go straight to any chapter and any section that looks the most rewarding. For example, if using an arts-based approach is what interests you, then go straight to Chapter 5; or, if you want to relocate the topic to another time period, then go to the 'New places and periods' section of Chapter 2.

Why do I not call this first stage 'blue-sky' thinking? It's a delightful image: sitting down with a blank sheet of paper and noting down fresh ideas that sprout from your fertile mind; or coming up with a whole bouquet of them from free-flowing conversation with friends. It may sound enticing, but for many students it's stony ground. 'Blue-sky' thinking only works when you have real familiarity with your topic (for example, when you have already done a lot of reading or can build on previous years of study). If you undertake 'blue-sky' thinking without background knowledge, you'll arrive at a list of topics that has little or no connection to the literature. This also tells us that if you are advanced in your studies, then 'blue-sky' thinking is more likely to work. Even then, I'd recommend reading as your starting point. Reading is the core technique for generating ideas. That's what many academics do. That's what I do. To make a contribution to the literature you have to start with the literature.

'Reading and generating ideas' depicts a sequence, or, more accurately, a cycle: you read, then you generate ideas, then you read again, generate better ideas, then you read again, etc. ... until your assignment is complete. To help ensure you are engaging with recent ideas you should focus your reading on more recent publications, such as those from the past 10 years or so. This timeframe is indicative rather than directive: it can be less and it can be more. It's worth noting that, sometimes, ideas have 'second lives'; the earliest references may be from 50 years ago but they have, for some reason, come round again, or become popular for the first time only recently. For example, the environmentalist theory of 'degrowth' was coined by André Gorz in the 1970s, but with the rapid and urgent rise of environmental concerns, it became the buzzword of a new debate in the 2020s.[1]

How can you identify the key claim to originality in a paper or book? This key claim will be there in a paper's title and/or abstract or in the title or on the first few pages of a book. Often it can be found in the blurb on the back of a book (the back blurb of academic monographs is usually written by the author). You are looking for the key words that summarise an innovation. For more on this see the 'How do you recognise new key words?' section of Chapter 3.

CASE STUDY

Discipline: Health and Social Care

Assignment: Write an essay on Health and Place

Innovative idea: 'Therapeutic geographies'.

In this scenario, students have been encouraged to offer a clear and specific argument. The overall topic already suggests that a geographical perspective might be useful. Having read 'New disciplinary contexts', one of the six ways of being original introduced in Chapter 2, you begin to search the combination of 'health', 'place', 'geography' and 'geographies' in an academic search engine. A brief survey of the first couple of pages of titles shows it's a diverse site of disciplinary connection and that several sub-fields are being mentioned, such as 'geographies of health' and 'hospital spaces'. However, let us say that it is 'therapeutic geographies' that stands out for you, both because it connects to your interests and because it appears most intimately concerned with the assignment topic of 'place' (you might also notice that 'therapeutic geographies' has overlap with the study of 'therapeutic landscapes'). This is also a promising candidate because the relevant articles are largely recent and none appear older than 15 years.

As the case study suggests, what you are searching for is a recent and innovative idea to work with, and a topic that does not get zero results – although that does happen – but results that are relatively few in number and relatively recent. The fact that just one, or a few, author names keep on cropping up connected with the idea is also a good sign, as these can provide your anchor authors. Scarcity in older sources but evidence of a lot of activity in recent years is another positive indicator. For example, 'therapeutic geographies' produces many more results recently than 10 years ago and, although there are quite a few (even with 'include citations' turned off, when I last looked there are 386), all the key ones are on the first several pages and the same authors feature repeatedly. Compare to 'human geography', which produces 822,000 results, from highly diverse authors, with many from a *really* long time ago (from the 1900s onwards).

NURTURING THE ORIGINAL IMAGINATION

There are different types of learners and different students need different forms of preparation for the exciting but initially daunting task of being original. For the most part, I take a mechanical approach: 'you do this and that follows'. This is fine for a lot of students, especially the more confident ones. But many will feel that they do not have the right 'mindset' to even begin original thinking. This is OK. It's the place where a lot of people start from. And it is understandable, especially in the context of the uncreative and rigid learning environments that many students will have endured in secondary education. Thus, a wider preparation is sometimes needed; a re-orientation towards the 'original imagination'. The educators Marten Scheffer, Matthijs Baas and Tone Bjordam (2017) have written about this nurturing process and I have adapted their ideas on the teaching of originality.[2] This list, derived from their work, includes provocations and points of reflection as well as practical pointers.

Collect diverse experiences: Original thinkers are open to the unplanned and the value of diverse experience; they are curious about what they don't know and what they have yet to experience. An attitude of curiosity towards the world is something to nurture and value. It often means that you prefer to listen than talk, that you find a wide variety of things interesting and that you are willing to admit that you don't know everything, or much at all!

Make empty time…: Scheffer et al. explain that 'distracting sounds and other uncontrollable stressors are negatively associated with creativity', but also that 'despite its negative connotation, boredom may provide fertile grounds for innovation'. They imply that a period away from tech – especially turning off one's smartphone – can be helpful. In our era of 'digital technologies, it may require slightly more effort than before to disconnect, but it is likely worth it', they write, adding that we should 'see the habit to make empty time as a way to create distraction-free episodes' that allow us to make sense of and 'process' our diverse experiences.

…but prime the mind: Scheffer et al. take the example of Darwin, 'who famously took walks along his especially constructed "thinking path"

every day without exception. He would usually have a particular problem in mind that he wanted to process over such walks'. Thus, they recommend doing something restful, quiet and that doesn't require much thought, such as going for a walk, while bringing the ideas you are working on with you and mulling them over, as a useful part of your everyday routine. Students, unlike Darwin, don't have a vast reserve of knowledge – their own private mind library – to transform a meander into a paradigm shift. But, nevertheless, the practice of 'making restful empty time but priming the mind' can be useful, even if it only involves giving yourself an hour or so of thinking time on a regular basis. A period away from distraction, away from screens and social media, can help reduce the noise of ordinary life and allow your thoughts to form and blossom.

Carry a notebook: Scheffer et al. remind us that 'the simplest of all habits is to always carry a notebook' and that ideas 'often come at inconvenient moments'. This is an excellent tip. Would-be original thinkers need to be prepared to jot things down at any time. It could be after you have read something, but equally it might happen during a TV programme or just as you are about to fall asleep. You never know when it will be, and if you wait, and don't note it down, you will probably forget it.

Take risks: Being original means going beyond the prescribed reading list and the expected topics. This is inherently risky and means leaving the comfort zone of 'doing what you're told'. But it's a calculated risk and a circumscribed one: you don't ignore the reading list but look at related reading and related topics. For Scheffer et al., 'mistakes are a calculated risk of innovation' and they advise that although 'far-fetched jumps' are not advisable, students need to be adventurous, pursuing themes that do not, at first glance, appear certain of any return.

Destroy your work if needed: Scheffer et al. point out that originality often takes a number of attempts to get right (and even then, it is unlikely to be perfect). Having the courage to say 'no this isn't working' and to redline what you have written is necessary for original outcomes. However, I would add another point: 'do not waste work'. In other words, even if an idea didn't work out, keep those references and don't delete that file. Create a space for it and keep it safe, as you never know when you may want to return to it.

Failing is necessary: Be prepared to admit disappointment, for example by admitting that your 'new idea' is not only not new but pretty common and becoming dated. It's a cliché but true: failure is the mother of invention. Samuel Beckett's gritty *cri de coeur* is also worth repeating:

(Continued)

'Try again. Fail again. Fail better.' If you do find that your topic or idea appears to be a dead end, you can either abandon it or adapt it, add some other theme or focus – perhaps by combining it with another innovation, and carry on. Failure comes in different flavours. Sometimes it is stark and absolute, but not always; it can be indeterminate and uncertain and, with work, there may still be a way forward.

Being part of a community of learners

You're not on your own. Students are part of a community of learners and that community includes all the authors of the articles and books you read and all the academics in your institution as well as all your fellow students. All of them are on the same journey, of exploring and finding out more. This is an important re-orientation: do not think about the world in terms of teachers, who have the knowledge, and learners, who don't, but rather as a commonwealth of scholars. This will also help you think about the authors you have to read, as well as the staff who lecture you, as real people and, in more practical terms, as resources for engagement. For example, when you are provided with a set reading, type the name of the author into a search engine and see what else they have written. To do so will shed light on the set reading; it will no longer appear like a final or fixed conclusion but as one moment, a stage on a journey. This re-orientation can also transform your relationship with your teachers. Taking a moment to look at the staff pages on a department or school website is a good idea. Knowing what interests your teachers and assessors and what they have written can provide all sorts of useful links, ideas and references. It also provides helpful background for talking to them about your own ideas.

2. Focusing and anchoring

Focusing refers to surveying the idea or ideas you have generated and picking out the one you want to go with. Anchoring refers to linking that chosen idea to a specific author or authors. The two often happen together but I'll explain focusing in more detail first.

The outcome of Stage 1 (reading and generating ideas) I outlined above is fed into Stage 2. This second phase can be thought of as deepening and giving precision to your ideas. You have to work out which of your ideas is the most promising.

A useful way of thinking about which of your ideas will work best is to summarise each in a pithy phrase or short sentence. This will help make clear whether or not they sound meaningful and promise valuable insight. This 'key statement' will be at the heart of your assignment and of your claim to originality. Try to make it focused and compelling but also serious. Claims to originality that are 'over the top' do not convince. The way you avoid this is through *qualification*. Look at the following three sentences:

> The gendered nature of regional policy is a relatively new area of study.
>
> This study aims to contribute to recent work on the gendered nature of regional policy.
>
> The gendered nature of regional policy has not been studied before, making the present study original.

The first two sentences are much more convincing than the last one. Why? The reason is that the first two contain qualifiers but the last does not. This is indicated by the fact that the first two use the words 'relatively' and 'aims to contribute'. There are many similar terms and phrases: for example, 'may be useful in...', 'can, in part, help to...'. Qualifiers mean you are holding back from an 'over the top', all-or-nothing claim, such as writing that a topic 'has not been studied before'. They tell us you have been reading, that you know the field and that your essay is an act of engagement. The third sentence sends out all the wrong signals because it has no qualifiers. It sounds arrogant and ignorant and it takes an unnecessary risk. No work *ever* been done? Are you sure? Qualifying your claims makes you sound serious and informed, and thus makes your argument more plausible.

Now let's look at 'anchoring'. Not all references are equal. Some are there to evidence a fact or the breadth of your knowledge. The anchor author (or authors) is different. This author (or authors) may have written the paper or book whose insights you are developing and/or they may be the person whose work you are critiquing. In either case you will be using this author or authors to ground your essay and explain its innovation. They can also be thought of as your ally (as discussed in 'Your allies' in the Introduction). For example, you may quote them to show that your topic, or your approach to it, is indeed a 'new field', 'emergent', 'under-researched' or some similar phrase.

CASE STUDY

Topic: Health and Place

Focus and anchor: A contribution to therapeutic geographies through an engagement with a paper by Karolina Doughty (2013).

You have identified the topic of 'therapeutic geographies' and found several pages of papers about it in an academic search engine. You have noted down a few potential leads but you are still presented with choices. For example, your focus might be therapeutic geographies in the context and aftermath of war, in hospital settings or in community farms. These are all topics that have appeared over the past 10 years or so and each is associated with specific authors. It would be possible to 'work with' any of them. Since they may all fit the bill, my advice is to be led by what interests you. Originality is all about engagement, so it is your concerns and passions that must drive it. Let's say that you are most attracted to a paper by Karolina Doughty (2013), which is about walking and therapeutic geographies and was published in the journal *Health and Place*.[3] The paper's abstract notes 'the lack of attention to embodiment and movement in work on therapeutic landscapes' and argues that 'shared movement can produce supportive social spaces that are experienced as restorative'.

> *Sample sentence*: Drawing on the work of Doughty on the embodied nature of therapeutic geographies, this essay argues that the connections between health and place require methodological and interdisciplinary innovation. More specifically, I examine methodologies for practising and researching 'place therapy' and show that, while they remain undeveloped, new work on 'walkscapes' and other forms of mobility ('swimscapes', 'runscapes', for example) can provide a helpful framework for future work.

In this sample sentence, an anchor author's breakthough is identified and supported but, importantly, it is clearly signalled that it is going to be developed. Doughty's work isn't just going to be repeated but expanded. The contribution will come in two ways: in connecting 'practising and researching' (the paper by Doughty you cite is focused on the former) and in pushing Doughty's methodology into new areas with new words (Doughty's term 'walkscapes' is picked out and expanded into 'swimscapes' and 'runscapes'). Chapter 4 is on methodological innovation and this will provide further tips on how you might build on Doughty's ideas.

TIP

Originality is not a hunt for the obscure

Originality is not found in inconsequential detail. It can be useful to explore minor themes and bring them to the fore (as discussed in Chapter 2) but there always needs to be substance to originality. This means that the topic or approach you are developing needs to be significant or have potential significance. It is usually necessary to anchor claims to significance through reference to scholarship.

---

3. Planning

Planning is about ensuring delivery. One of the common mistakes made in the pursuit of originality is to make a claim and not deliver it. If you can't deliver don't promise.

To ensure this doesn't happen you need to provide explicit evidence to support your claim to innovation. This requires that you use and return to the terminology you used in the key sentence you used at the start of your assignment and that your innovative argument is made at the start of an assignment and then developed in the body of the text and in the conclusion.

CASE STUDY

Topic: Health and Place

Planning: A 2000-word essay anchored in Doughty's (2013) work on walking and therapeutic geographies.

The 'focusing and anchoring' stage arrived at the key sentence we saw above ('Drawing on the work of Doughty on the embodied nature of therapeutic geographies, this essay argues…'). Now it is time to structure the essay to ensure this claim is delivered. In an essay of 2000 words, one simple way of planning the essay is as follows:

> *Introduction*: sets out the argument (with key sentence) and why it usefully contributes to wider debates in the health and place literature. Also sets out essay plan.

(Continued)

Section one: provides examples of Doughty's argument and makes reference to related health and place studies.

Section two: expands Doughty's argument by introducing the concepts of 'swimscapes' and 'runscapes'. Argues for the importance of connecting research and practice.

Conclusion: reasserts the central argument but also makes a wider argument for a 'turn towards diverse mobilities' in therapeutic geographies and health and place studies.

Note: Your structure can help you make sure that you tie your essay to the assignment topic of 'health and place'. The relevance of your focus on therapeutic geographies is not left to 'speak for itself' but is explained. Note also that the conclusion is not treated as an afterthought or mere summary. As well as using it to say 'this essay has shown', make the conclusion do real work, such as reinforcing but also expanding the nature and scope of your innovation, and telling the reader why it matters.

Planning also provides a moment to think about the possibility of introducing originality into how you write up an assignment. I am referring to how you divide up and compose your work. The topic of language use is addressed in Chapter 3 and illustration in Chapter 6. However, there are other innovative forms you can use, such as vignettes. A vignette is a short pen-portrait of something, such as a person, place or process. If placed appropriately in an essay – preferably after a more general discussion of the kind of issues that the vignette captures – such portraits can bring life and depth to your work. Vignettes are especially useful in longer work, in dissertations for example, where the word limit is more forgiving. It is useful to make clear to the reader why and how you are using vignettes. This means explaining that you will be using them in the Introduction and, perhaps, placing them in boxes.

Originality for different assessments

(For presentations, posters, podcasts and group work, see Chapter 6.)

As a rule of thumb, the more words you have been given to explore a topic the more space you have to be original. Multiple-choice exams allow no room for originality. Micro-assignments, where you are asked to write a few hundred words 'describing', 'outlining' or 'summarising' a topic, are little better. By contrast, when you have thousands of words to play with, originality can come to the fore. Another indication that you are being offered the chance to be original is the freedom given to you to choose your title and topic.

Dissertations, which might be 10,000 words or so and often allow students a choice of approach and subject, provide considerable scope for originality. However, originality, if approached correctly, is likely to be welcome and rewarded in essays and exams. Unlike dissertations and similar long-length assignments, essays and exams are unlikely to be bespoke: titles are often set and markers may be assessing a large volume of scripts. In these circumstances, it is important to keep claims to innovation simple and clear. A pressurised assessor who sees their job as making sure the 'question is answered' (and this is the core job of any marker) can be baffled – rather than impressed – by attempts to go off-piste and try out new ideas, especially if these ideas are not anchored in the literature. To avoid this, you should limit the scope of any innovation, for example by rooting it in just one new idea, firmly anchored in the literature, and presented upfront, in the first paragraph. As we have already seen, originality does not work if it is not delivered, so it is also necessary to mainstream your new idea, to return to it at various points in your text, including in the conclusion.

Traditionally, originality was not something expected of undergraduate students. It was imagined to be the preserve of the highest level of student scholarship, the PhD. It remains the case that for a PhD to be awarded it *has* to show a significant original contribution to its field. For taught postgraduate courses (such as MAs) and for undergraduate students, the expectations are lower. But originality is, nevertheless, widely written into assessment criteria at all levels. Moreover, there has been a wider shift towards understanding originality as a core aspiration of higher education. The further along in your studies you are the more creativity will be expected of you. This makes sense, but a purely incremental model, in which you are 'allowed' to become more ambitious with each new semester, should not limit your ambition or encourage you to see innovation as something you will 'get onto' when older. Originality is not a product of age but of engagement. Given the opportunity, any student, at any level, can make use of the techniques outlined in this book.

The politics of originality

One of the worries students have about originality is that they are entering a politicised environment whose cultural codes and expectations are unwritten and unclear. Such concerns are not universal but it is necessary to take them seriously.

I start with a paradox: the more authoritarian and conservative a society, or institution, the easier it is to be original. It does not take much, aside from courage, to be a pioneer when everyone around you must toe the line. This scenario also points to the global geography of originality. What might appear to be old-fashioned in one place may be bold in another. Readers in the 'freedom-loving' West may imagine I am depicting a contrast between them and everywhere else. One of the ways that Western culture has been defined is by its openness and innovativeness.[4] A flip side of this claim on innovation is that the existence and nature of the limits on originality in the West are hard to see and acknowledge.

These are general observations but they result in specific outcomes. Students in the West, when told, yet again, they should be enjoying the intellectual freedom available to them and that their ideas are valued, don't leap from their seats in excitement. They have heard it all before and they know the truth is not so straightforward. All institutions are conservative[5] but in different ways; some forms of originality are welcome, but not others.

The pathway through this uncertain terrain is to engage. Throughout this book I show that originality arises from engagement. If students are focusing and anchoring their work in the literature, they will, in effect, be being guided and aided by other scholars. Thus, the chances of taking a misstep, of giving offence or blundering, are minimised.

This is a neat solution to the problem and for some it will appear altogether too neat. The Canadian academic and former politician Michael Ignatieff is one of the most thoughtful of those commentators who worry about the death of originality in modern universities. He points to 'trends, fashions, movements and dogma', which he pins on various leftist theories that have created 'closed language games for initiates' and concludes that '[t]hinking for yourself in a university is not easy'.[6] Ignatieff's concerns channel wider stereotypes of modern universities as overtaken by 'wokeism', 'cancel culture' and liberal-left norms.

For students trying to navigate these issues, it is useful to distinguish giving offence from intellectual tolerance. It is a common excuse of those who wish to denigrate a liberal opinion or a minority group that they are free thinkers. However, academic originality has nothing to do with ill-informed or insulting rhetoric. Indeed, since it is an act of engagement, it tends in the opposite direction, towards understanding and empathy. What this tells us is that originality is not stymied by limitations on giving offence. But Ignatieff is not saying it is. He is pointing to the development of wider exclusionary norms and forms of 'group think'. I think he is wrong to imply that such trends are new: the idea that universities were once places of unhindered ideological diversity is a myth. Nevertheless, Ignatieff's argument retains its bite, especially for students who find themselves having to work out the opinions of academics who hold almost total power over their success and progress. There is no quick fix for this, but it is important not to pre-judge your teachers or your institution. A quick search online will establish their public convictions, or lack of them. My advice and my experience are that as long as you are engaging the literature and not seeking to give offence, you do not need to be anxious that your ambitions to originality will be rebuffed or 'cancelled'. However, I do not want to conclude this section with what might sound like a blandishment. Students are told that their ambitions matter and their ideas are valued. But few higher education institutions have yet to really fulfil this promise or acknowledge the range of consequences that flow from it.

Conclusion

> Originality is nothing but judicious imitation.
>
> Voltaire (attrib.)[7]

Voltaire was wrong. Originality builds on the work of others; it always refers back as well as forward. But if it was mere *imitation*, however 'judicious', it would be nothing more than repetition. Originality is an engagement: a 'building on' and a 'working with'. The shocking truth about originality is that it is real and within reach.

The form of preparation I have been discussing has been practical and has not shied from the fact that originality comes not from effortless brilliance, but from hard work and knowledge. Originality is not a routine expectation and it is important not to over expect. Don't beat yourself up if it doesn't happen in every assignment. No one is pushing forward all the time. It's OK not to be original. But it is also important to have the knowledge and confidence to know that originality is possible.

In this chapter the preparations for originality have been laid out. To put these preparations in place, students need to have some sense of the kind of argument they will be applying to their material. In other words, this is not a stand-alone chapter: to make full use of it you will need to take a look at at least one of the following five chapters.

2

Six Ways to Make Your Work Original

Introduction

Here are six straightforward techniques that can transform your work. Many researchers have built their careers through 'opening up' their field in the ways I will be outlining. At the end of this chapter I look at how you choose between them. You only need one. You don't become more original by doing 50 original things. You become baffling. Keep it simple. You'll get a sense of which one of these six approaches might work for you by reading through them all alongside the particular assignment criteria, title or topic you have to complete.

1. New places and periods

New places: Taking your topic elsewhere

I guess it is because I am a geographer that I am attracted to attempts to broaden topics by *relocating* them. When thinking about geographical contexts, two questions present themselves: where? (obviously) and (less obviously) 'according to who?'.

'Where?' can have many answers but a popular one is 'another country'. Your choice of country needs to be justified and justifiable. As a first step, type your key term, or key terms, plus the name of a country that you suspect will provide an interesting context, into an academic search engine. What you are looking for is an anchor author (someone who has written about your topic in relation to your country of choice) whose work you can engage and build on. Language skills and translation apps can be useful at this point. In many cases, moving beyond your preferred language is not essential or required, but it can assist in making your work original (see 'International languages and original words', Chapter 3).

Using a 'new place' as a new context requires an understanding that countries, especially larger ones, are diverse. Relocating a topic to India is a very different challenge from relocating it to Malta. Indeed, India is so diverse that it may be more plausible to focus on a smaller scale, such as a particular Indian state. On the other hand, some countries are so small, such as tiny island nations, that you may struggle to justify studying them at all. Anchoring your choice in the academic literature will help guide you. If you find yourself stuck in geographical channel-hopping – I'll do Thailand, no I'll do Panama, but how about Iceland? – it is likely you haven't anchored your work. As we have already learnt, originality is not about isolating yourself and thinking up utterly unique stuff, but an exercise in construction and connection.

Taking a 'new place' as your 'new context' relocates your topic and is going to require that you read about this place, to get to know it better. It also raises questions about perspective, i.e., we must ask 'according to who?'. Topics often look different according to *where* you study them from and every *where* has many points of view. For example, rather than simply relocating your topic to Morocco, you might want to think about how your object of study varies from the point of view of contemporary Moroccan novelists or Black Moroccans or women of Berber heritage. Another kind of focus is occupational and institutional. Writing about 'Moroccan town planners' or the 'Moroccan judiciary' is more useful than just writing about 'Moroccans'. These are all examples of *focus* and they are useful because they help avoid the problem of generalisation, i.e., implying that Morocco is undifferentiated and that all Moroccans have the same social roles and experiences and think alike.

Relocating a topic presents us with the challenge of comparison, for example, comparing China and India or India and the USA. Comparison can be an explicit and central aspect of your claim to be original. Comparisons work best when the two things you are comparing are similar but different (notice the countries I just mentioned are all big, diverse places); if there is little difference or little similarity then a comparison is likely to be pointless.

CASE STUDY

Topic: Gentrification

Assessment type: Exam

Title: 'Outline the causes and consequences of gentrification.'

Sample sentence: This essay argues that the principal causes of gentrification are deindustrialisation and housing shortage, while the main consequences are improved economic opportunities (for some) and the displacement of marginalised populations. Drawing on evidence from Japan, I show that these causes and consequences are internationally variable and that, in Japanese cities, although the causes are similar to those identified in the USA and Western Europe, the consequences have tended to be less disruptive and may be better framed as 'revitalisation'.

Note: In exams, you need to show you are answering the question upfront and early. But you can still be original. In this example the originality is communicated in the second sentence, which sticks to the question but adds to and informs the first sentence. Note also that since the question uses plurals – 'causes' and 'consequences' – you are expected to identify more than one of each.

TRY THIS

Take a specific topic from your course and type it into an academic search engine along with the name of a country, place or region that interests you. You may need to do this several times before you get useable results. Hopefully you will find not only a new geographical context, but an anchor author or authors.

New periods: Taking your topic to another time

Just as a new place can shed new light on a topic, so can a new period. Historical relocation can be combined with geographical relocation. Morocco in the early twentieth century or Morocco during the late colonial period sound a lot more plausible – because they are more specific – than simply 'studying Morocco'.

Historical reframing needs to avoid three dangers: *anachronism, eccentricity* and anything that *takes you away from your brief*. Anachronism is what happens when you take a topic outside the historical context that gives it meaning. For example, an essay on 'proletarian lives in ancient Egypt' takes a modern category – 'proletarian' – and transports it back to a period when it did not exist. It is true that, sometimes, originality can be a product of trying to question and rearrange historical assumptions about what concept fits what period. For example, there is a lively debate about the appropriateness of using the concept of racism in ancient societies. At least some historians have decided that this is an issue worth considering.

When taking your topic to another time, academic historians are your allies and your anchors. Engaging with them will also allow you to avoid the pitfall of eccentricity; in other words, any form of originality that appears arbitrary, disengaged and bizarre. If you can find one or more academic authorities (in a paper, chapter or book) that indicate that your decision to relocate your topic within a particular period is plausible and useful, then you will be on much firmer ground.

Just as a geographical reframing can adopt diverse scales and points of perspective, historical reframings can open diverse viewpoints. Your evidence, i.e., your source material, will guide and frame the nature of the viewpoint you are interested in. The more specific these sources and 'points of perspective' are the better. Let us take a nineteenth-century British example. Democratic, pro-suffrage, 'Chartist' newspapers were largely written from the perspective of the working class, and provide evidence of working-class experience and changing class relations. This is a specific source and topic, not a general allusion to what 'people thought'. These newspapers open up a particular and revealing worldview.

Time has rhythm and repetition. Categories like 'seasonal migration', 'daily life' or 'the working day' can also be approached as original contexts within which to examine a topic. Such contexts can open out the more intimate and ordinary aspects of history. However, as always, originality needs an anchor: you need to be clear about your source material and/or identify your academic ally/allies. Originality is not conjecture but grounded in evidence.

CASE STUDY

Topic: Globalisation

Assessment type: Essay

Title: 'Outline the relationship between trade and globalisation with reference to examples.'

Sample sentence: Drawing on the work of Green and Red, this essay will argue that globalisation has accelerated the homogenisation of trade. It also evidences the advantages of rethinking the history of this process by pointing to examples of how 'early' or 'archaic' globalisation (see Blue) evidence and pre-figure the homogenisation of 'international' trade.

Note: In this example, the originality is carried in the idea that the topic can be usefully located in the distant past. This idea is authorised by reference to academic studies ('Drawing on the work of …') and by having its key terms flagged in quote marks ('early' or 'archaic'), which suggests they have been drawn from reading.

TRY THIS

Aim: Explore the usage of a key term over time

Take a key term from an essay or dissertation title and enter it into a frequency or historical search engine, such as Google Ngram Viewer. This will show the volume of usage of the term from all sources in their archive over a range of years or decades. It can show revealing spikes and troughs in particular periods. You can click through to explore these highs and lows further. It is also useful to put your key term into other historical databases, such as Digital History or the Internet Ancient History Sourcebook.

2. New themes

There are many possible new contexts. Each requires that you focus and anchor to make sure your claim to be innovative is convincing. The more specific your context the easier it is to avoid generalisations. They sometimes emerge from combining topics. For example, let us imagine that your overall topic is pollution, and you decide, after focusing and anchoring the issue, that you are interested in attitudes among children towards pollution. However, your research has shown that a lot has been written about this topic. You need to navigate this sea of work and head towards a particular port. You find one or two intriguing studies which combine the topic with nutrition. This three-way combination (children's attitudes, pollution and nutrition) provides your harbour: it offers specificity, originality and a substantive research topic. An essay that combined these aspects would bring to bear more than one context and, by so doing, appear both focused and innovative.

CASE STUDY

Topic: Children's nutrition

Assessment type: Dissertation

Title: '"Moral panics" in childhood nutrition: A post-Western perspective.'

> *Sample sentence*: This dissertation draws on new work in post-Western sociology (Green; Brown) to critique and expand existing frameworks applied to media and politically generated 'moral panics' about poor nutrition and eating habits among school-aged children.

> *Note*: The innovative context of 'post-Western sociology' is flagged as a distinct and 'new' area of study. This context is anchored and employed to add value to an existing theme ('moral panics') within the study of child-hood nutrition. This original approach is boldly communicated in the dissertation sub-title.

TRY THIS

Aim: Generate a new theme

Take a paper or chapter from two different reading lists set for your course. Identify and note down the main innovative theme of each. Then combine them, using one as a prefix for the other. You may need to tinker with this for-mula, perhaps adding an additional term or rephrasing the key terms. Repeat the exercise with different papers or chapters until you have a selection of three or four new themes.

3. Minor to major

The themes that dominate debate today are usually ones that had a marginal existence in the past. What does this tell us? It suggests that many of the dominant themes of future study exist right now but within marginalia, i.e., footnotes, digressions and asides. You can hunt out new ideas in this material, pursue them further and, maybe, trans-form a minor comment into a significant agenda.

It would be easy to waste a lot of time truffling through footnotes hoping to snout out something of value. Ideally, discovering a minor item that has potential for being expanded and developed happens as a side-product of your normal work; you just need to be alert to the possibility. So what are you looking for? Which details, which minor themes, have the makings of something 'major'? Occasionally, this potential is explic-itly flagged by authors as significant but beyond the remit or capabilities of their study. But usually you have to use your own judgement.

You want to avoid themes that are conjectural, vague and/or do not point to matters of substance. To see what this means let us look at examples.

1. A footnote that suggests that the least affluent Moroccans cannot read French, although French remains the language of choice for most profession-als in Morocco. This is a significant topic; it is suggestive of issues of cross-cultural literacy, colonialism and social exclusion. It might be worth exploring and, depending on your area of study, it might be original.
2. A couple of asides (digressions in a narrative): one suggests Morocco is a patriarchal society; the other that there are now 18 TV channels in the king-dom. Neither gives us much to go on: one is a well-known generalisation; the second is an isolated fact. Neither would provide a solid starting point for original enquiry. Themes that are worth taking from minor to major need to be capable of 'opening-up' your topic and pointing towards the existence of a specific pathway through it.

CASE STUDY

Topic: Pre-school learning and environmental education

Assessment type: Dissertation

Title: 'After nature? Rethinking environmental learning among pre-school children.'

Sample sentence: Brown identifies the core challenges facing environ-mental learning among pre-school children as safety, resources and educator/carer skills. However, Brown has acknowledged [in a footnote] that the absence of wider 'environmental experience' among young people does much to explain the nature and context for her study. In this dissertation, it is shown that, although it remains a marginal theme in the literature (see Blue; Yellow), the decline or perceived absence of 'nature' in both children's and educators' lives should be foregrounded in research on environmental education.

(Continued)

Note: Academic authorities are used here to evidence that the topic to be explored is important but is currently marginal within the research literature. The title of the dissertation uses a question mark and the word 'rethinking' to communicate original intent. This example also shows how a 'taken-for-granted' theme – something that has been assumed but not interrogated (in this case 'environmental experience') – can be taken from 'minor to major'.

TRY THIS

Aim: Expanding a footnote

If a chapter, book or paper from one of your reading lists has footnotes, take a look through them. Do any of them jump out as having further potential and as being substantive? If so, explore them further with an academic search engine. You are testing to see if this 'minor' topic might be worth expanding. If you cannot find any footnote references that look to be likely candidates, try taking a paper or chapter (not a book, you want to keep this brief) and try to scan-read it for topics that are interesting and substantive but appear only once or briefly. You are on the hunt for phrases and themes that pop out as distinctive and digressive. 'Scan-reading' can be tricky; you haven't failed because nothing has 'popped out'. After all, you've just read a paper that is relevant to your field. Whatever happens, you haven't wasted your time.

4. New disciplinary contexts

Bringing in insights from another discipline provides one of the most common ways of being original. This version of originality shows, once again, that being innovative is not about blue-sky thinking or dispensing with tradition but connecting with other people's ideas.

It is necessary to be clear about what discipline or, even better, what specific sub-field you will be drawing on and to justify it. Sentences such as 'This essay draws on the emerging sub-field of Island Studies' or 'In this presentation I will be drawing on insights from cultural anthropology' indicate that your work is going beyond the usual and hints at why (because it is 'emerging', because of 'insights'). Notice that these sentences point to specific fields. This is more useful than, for example, claiming to be drawing on 'insights from philosophy'. Philosophy is extremely diverse, so 'insights from philosophy' sounds vague and ill-informed. Where possible, be specific and, of course, anchor. For example, 'This essay draws on the emerging sub-field of Island Studies, with particular reference to the work of Rose and Pink'.

Here are three more tips:

1. When bringing in other disciplines or sub-fields, *one is usually enough*. If they are at all substantial, one such field will provide sufficient direction and material.
2. *Do not stray too far*. Your discipline has related or cognate disciplines: many historians are broadly on the same page as cultural anthropologists but clinical psychology might baffle them.
3. Finally, *show knowledge*. Just having one reference to one paper from an 'emerging sub-field' is not enough. You need at least a few, so as to provide evidence that this is indeed an 'emerging' area and/or you have reliable knowledge of it.

CASE STUDY

Discipline: Urban Planning

Assessment type: Essay

Title: 'How urban redevelopment impacts community cohesion.'

Sample sentence: In this essay I will be drawing on recent work in urban cultural geography (Green; Orange) to argue that new forms of community cohesion can be and are created in the wake of what Blue calls 'inclusionary and diverse' forms of urban development. This argument also suggests that accounts, developed in urban planning research from the 1960s (see, for example, Red; Black), in which the impacts of urban development are generalised as destructive and deracinating, can and should be challenged.

Note: The author's discipline is urban planning so the original aspect being flagged in this sentence is that they will be drawing on the insights from 'urban cultural geography'. But it's not a step too far because human geography and urban planning are related fields. References to this new work – the 'urban cultural geography' – should be recent ones (they have to be, as you are claiming it is new), while those that relate to the approach that is critiqued, and 'developed … from the 1960s', will be older.

TRY THIS

Aim: Thinking about other disciplines

We all start off as interdisciplinary. Before you chose your current course you probably thought of alternatives. Dip back into one or more of those, making use of an academic search engine and the key words of the topic you need to write about. Use the 'search from' time limit function to avoid dated material. Try to find a named sub-field within this other discipline (for example, not just 'history' but 'post-colonial history'). Note down the following two things that can be applied to your topic and discipline: (a) a sub-field; and (b) some anchor authors.

5. New theoretical contexts

A theory is an argument that points to a wider explanation. 'People in my neighbourhood are rich' is not a theory. 'People in my neighbourhood are rich because they inherited wealth' is a theory (albeit a very basic one). Scaling up this idea, we can understand why general, explanatory arguments about social, cultural and natural processes can produce influential theories.

Theoretical innovation occurs in many ways. However, one of the most productive is via collision. Mixing and splicing theoretical traditions can enable a more sophisticated, as well as a pioneering, way of exploring a particular topic. Many celebrated theories arose from this process. Kimberlé Crenshaw's (2017) discussions of intersectionality or Immanuel Wallerstein's (2004) world systems theory all derived from creatively blending existing approaches.[1] They may seem rather grand illustrations but, at root, this is not a process that is necessarily daunting or complex. My two examples, with their attached labels ('intersectionality' or 'world systems theory') and attached names (Crenshaw and Wallerstein), also remind us of an important point when working with theory: a theory has a *label* and it is *someone*'s argument. No 'ism' speaks for itself. You are in conversation, not with an 'ism', but with human beings, who are themselves in conversations with other human beings. We need to know who they are.

A straightforward way in which you can be theoretically innovative is by saying that you have identified a theory which, while not new itself, is new in your area of study and has a contribution to make to it. For example, although geography is a theoretically diverse subject, there has been little work originating from a psychoanalytical perspective. The question thus becomes 'What contribution could such a perspective make to the study of geography?' As it turns out, and as some recent writers have come to accept, there are a range of insights that psycho-analysis provides on such issues as urban form and cultural landscape.

The pursuit of theories that have a possible contribution to your discipline or sub-field should not be undertaken for its own sake. Dragging in irrelevant and/or half-understood material merely because it appears novel is a bad idea and it will probably make your work incomprehensible. To avoid this danger, be specific and focused with your choices. We can return to the example of geography and psychoanalysis to see how. Psychoanalysis is a huge field, with many traditions and, unless you have a strong background in it, it is easy to get lost. Rather than just 'drawing on psychoanalysis', it would be more convincing to, for example, 'draw on Blue's work on psychoanalysis and architecture' or 'Green's recent studies of post-colonial psychoanalysis'. Citing and developing the trajectory of a named anchor author or authors will provide clarity, purpose and direction.

CASE STUDY

Topic: Sustainable development

Assessment type: Exam

Title: 'With reference to examples, outline and discuss the limits of sustainable development.'

> *Sample sentence*: This essay draws on the work of Blue and Silver to argue that the principal limits on sustainable development are structural inequalities. It frames these limits in terms of what Yellow calls 'every-day politics', an approach that draws out the lived, iterative and 'banal' nature of the way inequalities are reproduced and shape development.

Note: The first sentence makes it clear to the marker that you are answering the question. It does point to theory but not to theories that, in this field, would be seen as original. The theoretical originality is delivered in the second sentence and anchored by reference to a named author and a named idea ('everyday politics'). This innovation is clearly framed as complementing and contributing to the idea introduced in the first sentence: it is not just added on top of it but connected to it. Notice that the word 'theory' is not to the fore in this example, nor does it mention an 'ism'. Both tend towards generalisation and should be used only when absolutely necessary. In most cases, there is no need for either. It is clear from the framing – 'an approach that draws out the lived, iterative and "banal" ...' – that what is being offered is an original theoretical context.

> ## TRY THIS
> ### Aim: Looking for an innovative theory in titles
>
> Use the time limit function on an academic search engine to freely explore the titles of papers or chapters on your set topic published over the past 10 years or so. Don't be too strict with the timeframe (articles up to 15 or even 20 years old can be OK). What you are looking for are new theoretical themes that you can adopt and adapt for your own use and which are signalled in the title. Usually, the new theory will not come as an 'ism' (it can take decades for a new theory to become an 'ism'). It may be badged as an 'approach' or 'perspective', or use similar words that hint at the kind of general and explanatory level you are looking for (remember: a theory is just a form of argument). You are looking for ONE theory but it will be useful to note down a few, so you can choose between them. A short-cut is to search for 'new approaches in' or 'new theories in' your field or to find an overview article that summarises recent developments in your field.

6. Listening for absences and turning things around

A familiar component of everyday arguments is the assertion that what someone is *not* saying is just as important, and indeed more revealing, than what they *are* saying. This idea is just as common within academic debate. Listening for absences, for unspoken assumptions, can provide powerful critiques and enable the identification of substantive new areas of enquiry. Listening for absences is not the same as finding *gaps* in knowledge. Just because a topic has not been 'done' does not provide a rationale for why it should be. Listening for absences is about locating something that should be acknowledged because it has significance for an existing field or line of enquiry.

It is important to scope out whether others have already noted an absence before making use of it yourself. This scoping should not lead to you giving up just because someone has 'got there first'. It is about gaining knowledge that will help shape your contribution. For example, although pointing to the series of silences around the subject of gender and women in the work of the scholar of orientalism Edward Said may lead towards an interesting essay, many people have already noticed this absence.[2] 'Listening for what is not being said' is a familiar academic technique, so it is often the case that your attempt at it will, in some way, be derivative. This implies not that you give up, but that you need to acknowledge this prior work and focus and qualify your own claim. You can 'add value' to an existing critique by bringing further specificity to it, for example, by building on previous work on Said's silences around gender by focusing on peasant women or masculinity, terms which help define your intervention and clarify what it is adding.

'Turning things around' is another specific but potentially effective way of offering a challenge to conventional assumptions. If we look at an example we can see why. Consider the explanation of poverty in the 'Third World'. The traditional 'Western explanation', developed during the colonial era, was that poverty was caused by inadequacies within other cultures and that colonial contact was necessary in order to assist in the development process. However, this position was challenged by being 'turned around'. The new idea was that it was Western colonialism that caused the poverty: that it 'underdeveloped' the 'Third World'. Western colonialism was not the solution but the cause.[3] It is a large-scale illustration, but there are many such cases where *assumptions* about cause and effect can be identified and flipped. To take another instance, it is widely assumed that obesity is caused by over-eating. However, we can turn this around by framing over-eating as an outcome (perhaps of obesity itself or of other factors, such as environmental circumstances) rather than a cause.[4] What such examples teach us is that the effectiveness and utility of 'turning things round' depends on: (1) being able to identify and challenge an existing and dominant causal assumption; and (2) being able to explain why the reasoning behind this assumption is inadequate and, in some way, back to front.

CASE STUDY

Discipline: Psychology

Assessment type: Essay

Title: 'The psychology of old age and ageing.'

Sample sentences:

Listening for an absence:

In this essay it is argued that the psychology of old age and ageing remains dominated by Western models (see Red for discussion) and that, as issues of ageing and old age become increasingly important globally, a new post-Eurocentric and more diverse approach is needed.

(Continued)

Turning things around:

It has been assumed that ageing and old age frame and shape psychological problems and processes for older people (see Brown; Pink). In this essay it is argued that the causal power of 'ageing' and 'old age' has been exaggerated, or simply assumed, and that a range of cultural, environmental and psychological factors frame and shape the social construction of both terms.

TRY THIS

Aim: Identifying an absence

Take a key reference – a set book, chapter or paper that your lecturers have told you is important – and read it for what it fails to include. As an exercise, this works best if you just run at it and write down as many things – themes, topics, ideas – you can think of. Then you can look at your list and pick out those that you think might matter. You want to delete those items that aren't useful, in the sense that they won't open up the topic in a way that makes a difference. How do you know? In large part, it is educated guesswork and that's OK. It's more important that you get ideas down on paper than that everything is verifiable or correct. Often your 'keepers' will be broader themes, such as 'gender', that can be used to critique this 'key reference'. The next step is to do an online search for authors who have had the same idea. If there are hundreds or more, then move on. It's fine if there are none, but even better if there are a handful, as they can anchor your intervention. You should, if you decide to take your idea forward, engage with their work.

Conclusions: How to choose?

I have presented six ways of being original. Other innovative approaches are introduced in the next chapters. How do you choose which one is right for you? Three points will help.

1. *What fits*: Not all of these approaches will fit your work or the terms of your assessment. What you are looking to do is to make a sensible and useful intervention. Avoid anything that smacks of eccentricity or is veering off-piste. If you've been asked to write an essay on psychological theories in a course which has been all about *modern* psychological theories, then, unless you've

talked to the course leader and got the thumbs up, doing a presentation on medieval psychological thought is likely to be seen as misunderstanding what is required.

2. *Be guided by your anchor authors*: It is nearly always useful to anchor your endeavours in the work of others. This will also help determine your choice of 'new context' and can act as a spring-board, allowing you to develop, and perhaps critique, their work.

3. *Be guided by your interests and skills*: Originality is rewarding not simply because it can get high marks, but because it reflects your passions and personality. These may be long-held and close to your heart or, perhaps, reflect something that you can bring to the topic (for example, an occupational background or knowledge of a language).

3

Original Words

Introduction

In this chapter we look at how fresh, thought-provoking words and phrases can make your work original. The first part is about how you can identify key words and then adapt them. The second part introduces other ways in which you can use language to be innovative. We look at metaphors and similes, words from other languages, and the style and form of written work. There are many ways in which a bit of creativity in any of these areas can take your assignments to a new level. I'll be providing lots of examples and sample sentences. These will help you make choices about what may work for you and what won't. Finally, I look at how you can invent your own 'neologisms'.

Originality is nearly always communicated by key words that encapsulate a new field, approach or topic. If you think of any original idea – from the theory of 'quantum mechanics' to the 'decolonialised curriculum' – you will find a key word or phrase at the heart of it. These words deliver the idea: they sum it up. And they are *key* words: they open the door to new horizons.

When I first heard the expression 'moral panic', now much used by sociologists and many others, I was interested. It was a pithy encapsulation – a useful simplification – of a more complex idea; namely that the media were creating demonised targets to both explain and distract from wider problems of social decline. In part what impressed me was how succinctly those two words, 'moral panic', delivered this concept. Key words do important work: they tell us the essence of the argument, they organise its central principles and they proclaim to the world that an innovative concept has arrived.

Most 'new words' are seen as new for years after their first usage. This is good news for students because it tells us that you don't need to invent your own new key word or phrase. It is just as effective, and less risky, to work with an existing one (as long as it is still breaking new ground in your area of study). So you do not need to be snatching up this week's copy of *The Journal of Soft Fruit Studies* to get the freshest buzz terms in Soft Fruit Studies. It takes time – years, even decades – for new words to become routinised, standard and, perhaps, quietly discarded.

TIP

Pick one

It is usually far more effective to pick ONE new key word or phrase to work with than try to give equal weight to many. Occasionally connecting two can also work. You should identify the new term early on. In an exam or essay, this means naming, defining and anchoring it (via references) in the first or second paragraph, and then coming back to it several times, including in your conclusion.

Working with innovative key words

Innovative key words are ubiquitous. Nearly all published academic work contains them. But what do they look like? To illustrate 'new key words' we can group them under two headings: (1) words that depict *new theories and topics*; and (2) words that point to *new disciplinary fields*. You may notice that these titles are call-backs to headings featured in Chapter 2. In fact, 'new words' are central to the communication and currency of all forms of originality.

New theories and topics

New theories are encapsulated in new words. Here are three examples: the theory of 'non-representational theory' was developed by Nigel Thrift and others in the 1990s; 'accelerationism' was first coined by Benjamin Noys in 2010; and 'tipping point' (in the sense of climatic tipping points) comes from a 2008 paper called 'Tipping elements in the Earth's climate system'.[1] People hadn't heard these terms before but they were chosen because they were intriguing and pithy. And they stuck. Although now decades old, all three of these *labels* (which is another way of thinking of 'new words') are still being debated, and 'working with' them could be an original thing for students, at any level of study, to do.

Sample sentences:

This essay will be drawing the work of 'non-representational theory' (Thrift, 1996) into conversation with accelerationist perspectives (Noys, 2010).

In this essay I will be arguing that the field of social psychology can be usefully challenged and interrogated by drawing on theories of accelerationism (Noys, 2010).

It is shown that the climatic 'tipping point' has parallels in the study of biodiversity.

All three of these sentences make it clear that you are not just taking a 'new word' 'off the peg' and waving it about. You are *working with it*, engaging and adding. This does not mean it is wrong to write 'This essay will be using non-representational theory to explore...'. This is straightforward and might be the start of a good essay. Good but not original. Solid but not excellent. It takes an idea and plonks it down, unrefined and undigested.

Let's look at another example. Richard Florida's (2002) concept of the 'creative class' was an innovative social categorisation that identified 'creatives' as being key to urban change.[2] We can work with this expression by slightly expanding it, making it longer and more specific by adding one or two words.

Sample sentence: In this essay I discuss the 'racialised creative class', forcing an encounter between Florida's category and the racial politics of contemporary American cities.

In this sample sentence, an existing, well-known, new term ('creative class') is engaged, expanded and challenged. However, you don't have to invent your own combinations. Instead you can make use of existing adaptions. Let's take the example of 'world systems theory', a Marxist theory of global change developed by Immanuel Wallerstein in the 1970s. In the 1990s Alf Hornborg and others developed 'Ecological World Systems Theory'.[3] It's a new departure and, given our pressing environmental crisis, it still remains fresh. So fresh, in fact, that we could co-opt it and still deliver an original intervention. The sentence 'This essay will take a World Systems Approach (Wallerstein) ...' is fine, but not original. Compare it to 'This essay will take an Ecological World Systems Approach (Hornborg)'. Immediately, a sense of focus, or 'working with', comes into play, even though, in this case, all one is doing is hitching a ride on someone else's originality.

How do you recognise new key words?

They often have pride of place: in the title of a chapter, paper or book. Let's look at three of the titles of the books on the shelf in front of me. Can you spot the new key words? I've been writing on racial and ethnic studies for a long time, so that explains why they are all on this topic:

Critical Multiculturalism: Rethinking Multicultural and Antiracist Education (edited by Stephen May, 1999)

Embedded Racism: Japan's Visible Minorities and Racial Discrimination (by Debito Arudou, 2015)

Psychedelic White: Goa Trance and the Viscosity of Race (by Arun Saldanha, 2007)[4]

The 'new words' that these authors employ are the centrepieces of their books, their nutshell contribution, and they are there in their titles. Let's pull them out:

Critical Multiculturalism

Embedded Racism

Psychedelic White and *Viscosity of Race*

All the other words in these three titles are descriptive and conventional. But the ones listed above are different. In each case the key term is made by adding an adjective to a well-known noun and it is that combination that creates the original idea. *Critical Multiculturalism* is more than yet another book on multiculturalism. It claims to have a new take, what it calls *critical* multiculturalism, an idea that is defined in and returned to throughout the book. *Embedded Racism* is more than just another book about racism. That key term is telling us the author has a particular theory, in this case that racism is woven into Japanese society so deeply that it goes unnoticed. *Psychedelic White* and the *Viscosity of Race* are pointing to something even more ambitious. The title tells us that the author has both an original idea and an original topic. He gives a label, 'psychedelic White', to a specific form of whiteness: a trippy, hippy, vacation whiteness. The author doubles down on his claim to originality with a second term, which promises a controversial new theory of race. His reference to the 'viscosity of race' runs counter to the conventional social science position on the topic, namely that race has no material reality because it is a social construction. Saldanha is arguing that race does have a material reality, albeit of an odd kind, a sticky, clinging physicality (thus, he says, it is not an imagined or mythical thing but 'viscous').

If you are a student who wants to 'work with' these topics, what you need to do is engage and build.

> *Sample sentence*: Throughout this talk I have tried to explain the opportunities that Arun Saldanha's notion of the 'viscosity of race' provides to historical research on French abolitionism.

When it comes to originality, new words do a lot of the heavy lifting. As the intriguing but rather hyperbolic expressions 'psychedelic White' and 'viscosity of race' imply, there has been a tendency for ever more striking and rhetorically bold new composites. For example, 'disaster capitalism', 'zombie capitalism', 'hyper-capitalism' became *au courant*. Perhaps they go too far, turning theories into intellectual eye-candy. But the allure of language matters. Creating a new term is not only about creating an accurate encapsulation: 'new words' need to roll off the tongue and weave a spell.

The value of 'post'

A popular way of devising a new academic term is to bolt the adjective 'post' to the front of a noun. 'Post' has been added to a wide range of theories and topics in order to signal that a new idea has arrived. Post-truth, post-Western, post-socialism, post-structuralism, post-modernism are all terms that flag a critical engagement with and, in some way, a moving on from what has gone before.

The 'post' prefix contains an inherent claim to originality. But be careful. Some of the 'posts' still knocking about went out of fashion decades ago. Post-modernism is a good example. It was all the rage in the 1980s. 'Post-modern' was *everywhere*. However, this very popularity provoked a pushback, a revulsion against the new norm. Post-modernism became a victim of its own success and nothing looks more dated than the recently but no longer fashionable. In practical terms, this means that any student assignment that starts by claiming to 'take a post-modern approach' will not be seen as original; indeed, quite the opposite, this choice is likely to be seen as behind the times. In Chapter 1 I explained how you can tell when a new idea is no longer being seen as original. These tips apply just as well to new words. If you typed 'critique of' or 'anti' alongside 'post-modernism', you will find plenty of evidence that this is a 'new word' whose day in the sun came and went; intense but brief.

Not all 'posts' are equally current or equally useful. However, they are constantly rolling off the intellectual production line and searching them out can lead to innovative outcomes. One long-odds tip is simply to write 'post' in front of the key term you need to write about and see if you can find it being employed, from the last 10 years or so. You need to write an essay on gentrification? Search for 'post-gentrification' and – at least in this case – there it is; indeed, there is a debate centred on this concept. It took you 15 seconds to make that search but it could make all the difference: suddenly, you are in the driving seat, your essay transformed into something that is focused and up to date. Other examples include the Anthropocene and the West. A lot of people are talking about the post-Anthropocene, while recent years have witnessed the development of discussion on post-Western politics and sociology. Then there is 'post-sustainability', 'post-ecology'... I could go on. If you want to invent your own 'post', see the section on 'Inventing your own words' at the end of this chapter.

Using 'beyond' and 'after'

'Post' implies you have a clear programme. It may be a more definite and bolder claim than you want and, if so, a term like 'beyond' or 'after' can be useful. For example, in the corridors of my department this week I see they are advertising a talk titled 'Beyond post-colonialism'. It's not post-post-colonialism. Two 'posts' in a row looks silly. But that is not the main reason 'beyond' was being used. 'Beyond' and 'after' carry a different message. They suggest the speaker or author is going to raise some questions and probably introduce some new directions. This is more open-ended than 'post'. 'Beyond' and 'after' do not claim a new paradigm, but rather the promise of critique.

Whatever prefix you choose, you have to deliver. I went to that talk on 'Beyond post-colonialism' and left frustrated, as did everyone else I spoke to afterwards, because the speaker didn't deliver on the promise of the title. Indeed, the theme of 'beyond post-colonialism' was barely mentioned. It is a basic and easily avoided error: do not set up expectations and then fail to follow through.

New fields

Academic disciplines often produce new fields of enquiry. The most important way young academics forge their careers is by creating or contributing to a new field. These new fields have their own labels. The new fields of 'transcultural economics', of 'big data history', of 'carceral education studies' are like named brands and there will be some key authors associated with their creation and development. Engaging with a new field involves naming it and its key authors and explaining how you are contributing to it. It is important to make it clear that you are doing more than simply describing and repeating. As we have seen, originality is an active state: it is not passive reflection but a moulding, shaping and pushing forward.

Sample sentences:

In this essay I draw on the new field of 'critical behaviour studies' (Blue; Green) to show that ...

I argue that although the recently developed field of 'existential history' (Red; Brown) provides a compelling new framework to understand ..., the topic continues to be simplified and misrepresented.

TRY THIS

Aim: Finding new words

Go into a research search engine and type in your topic plus one or two words that might help you track down some of the new labels that are current in your field. These include 'new', 'new term', 'post-', 'beyond', 'recently' and 'neologism'. You will probably need to play around with a few such combinations. Use the 'custom range', or other time limit function, to limit your search to the last five years. You don't need to look beyond the titles of papers, chapters or books. After 20 minutes you should have arrived at one or two likely candidates, or concluded that you need to change how you express your topic and/or that you need to expand your search to abstracts and have a wider timeframe. You may decide the topic is not going to yield any results. The candidates you do find may be new 'isms', new composites or new sub-fields. This exercise is about finding such terms, so you can stop at this point, especially if none of the results interest you. But if something catches your attention, keep mining, you might strike gold.

Language tips for original thinking

Metaphors and original thinking

'He is drowning in money' and 'she's feeling blue' are metaphors. A metaphor is a figure of speech that swops a literal description with something more imaginative (in the two examples 'has a lot of' is swopped for 'is drowning in' and 'sad' for 'blue'). A metaphor is a way of encapsulating and explaining something in a creative, ingenious and compelling way.

Let's look at the example of 'genetic code'. You may wonder, 'is that a metaphor? Isn't that just a fact, a description of genes?'. Not at all. Genes are not, literally, a form of 'code', nor do they contain 'code'. Code is encrypted information. Genes no more contain code than the movement of the planets contains code, or the motion of the waves. 'Genetic code' is a metaphor. And it's a good one. It communicates, explains and sums up a complicated topic and it does it so well that people have lost sight of the fact that it is a metaphor or that it was ever invented. The metaphor of inherited 'code' was created by the physicist Erwin Schrödinger in 1944. He explained:

> [i]n calling the structure of the chromosome fibres a code-script, we mean that the all-penetrating mind ... could tell from their structure whether the egg would develop, under suitable conditions, into a black cock or into a speckled hen, into a fly or a maize plant, a rhodo-dendron, a beetle, a mouse or a woman.[5]

The metaphor of 'code' does a lot of work here: it captures what chromosomes do and how. It also offers us an intellectual framework to go further. For example, it implies that the 'code' can be 'broken', i.e., written out and understood, and thus the 'mystery' of inheritance can be revealed.

Metaphors matter. How can students make use of them in ways that are original? The answer is 'in the same way they can work with other new words' – with one difference: showing an understanding that this form of 'new word' *is* a metaphor – that its insight is based on an identification of one thing with a very different thing – is helpful and will shape the way you engage with it. We can look at another example to explain this.

The term 'cultural capital' reimagines cultural knowledge and power (for example, knowing another language or speaking with an 'educated' accent) as a form of economic asset (that is, as 'capital'). Pierre Bourdieu coined the term in the mid-1970s, and it is now a staple part of the social science lexicon.[6] It's no longer original, but it is still much discussed. So, if you 'worked with' the term – engaging recent debates and, by doing so, added to the term or adapted it – your work might well be seen as original. One of the ways you can do this is by expanding the term, for example, 'green cultural capital' or 'religious cultural capital'. Another way forward is to think about how 'cultural capital' works as a metaphor, more specifically, exploring, and perhaps critiquing, the way the topic you are concerned with *can* be understood and depicted as a fiscal asset. We might ask, for example, 'has capitalism changed today, so that "cultural capital" now carries new implications?', or 'does the image of capital provide a simplistic, economically reductive, model for understanding [my topic]?'.

It is hard to underestimate the importance of metaphors in understanding the world. In different eras, society has been understood as an organism, a system, a performance, a theatre, a machine, a network. All of these are metaphors, some current and some dated. 'Working with' the more recent of these metaphors can result in profound insights. But a word of caution is also necessary. Not all metaphors are equal. Some are little used or merely decorative. There is no point in engaging a metaphor that is mentioned in passing but is not central to an author's argument. The importance of a metaphor is indicated by its widespread use, by its place in the title of a paper or book, and by the way an argument relies on it.

A more general note of caution is also worth voicing. It is useful to ask, 'what is the real point, the aim, of using a metaphor?'. If it is not to understand better the thing that the metaphor is supposedly shedding light on (whether it be genetics or society or any other topic), but an end in itself, then you might be accused of getting lost in semantics or 'word spinning'. The linguist Noam Chomsky (1997) was warning against this danger when he wrote:

> metaphors are metaphors. If they're a stimulus to the imagination, fine. Let your imagination be stimulated. But one should not confuse metaphors and imaginative leaps with understanding; they may be a help to understanding, but then we await the understanding to make judgments. ... Use whatever metaphor happens to help you to think, but don't confuse the metaphor with a conclusion.[7]

Is Chomsky right? No and yes. Developing and refining a metaphor can give us a better picture of our topic; it can make us think more deeply about, for example, genetics or cultural power. Nevertheless Chomsky's words offer a useful steer. The point of engaging metaphors, and 'new words' more generally, is not to perfect the way we describe the world, but to know the world better.

TRY THIS

Aim: Looking for metaphors

This exercise is based on the reading list provided for a course you need to complete an assignment for. Can you identify metaphors in any of the titles of these set readings? It is especially useful if these metaphors can be found in

(Continued)

core texts and appear to be central to an author's argument. Sometimes there aren't any, or least they don't swim into view easily. This may be disappointing, but the point of this exercise is to get us to start looking for them – to notice the work they do – so even a nil result will not be a waste of time. If you can locate even just one metaphor, note it down along with one or two simple ways it might be helpful or misleading – for example, if it usefully makes us think of related processes (remember how 'genetic code' makes us think of 'code breaking') or if it suggests comparisons which are helpful or, alternatively, distort the topic.

International languages and original words

Academic writing often makes use of key words from other languages. These terms express something that is not easily expressed in one's own language and/or they point to a particular tradition or school of work. There is a bit of 'cultural capital' here too: using a term from another language can make you appear knowledgeable.

You do not need to be fluent to make use of other languages. I have schoolboy French that, traumatised by holiday encounters, my daughter says 'is the most embarrassing thing a human ear could hear'. But that doesn't stop me. I make use of French terms in my academic writing not because I am pretending to be bilingual, but because they accurately reflect a topic and its specific traditions. To grasp this point, it is useful to look at some other examples.

Gemeinschaft and *gesellschaft* refer, respectively, to traditional and modern social relationships: the former bonded through tradition and the latter held together through civic and legal association. These classic sociological terms arose from late nineteenth-century German sociology and they remain in use both because they encapsulate a distinction that still matters and because they point to a specific intellectual tradition (associated with Ferdinand Tönnies).[8] Among the world's living languages, German has produced the most academic loan-words. Others include *verstehen* (understanding/interpreting subjective meaning), *dasein* (existence), *gesamtkunstwerk* (total work of art) and *unheimlich* (uncanny).

Untranslated terms are also adopted because they refer to a specific ideology or practice rooted in a particular part of the world. For example, in the Spanish speaking parts of Latin America, the ideology and practice of 'race mixture' is called *mestizaje*. It's an evocative term that communicates much more than 'race mixture'. Therefore, English language scholarship on 'race mixture' in Latin America will usually be framed as a discussion of *mestizaje*.

Some words are said to be untranslatable. This is because they are embedded in a distinct, complex and culturally specific context. For example, *moksha* is a spiritual term in Hinduism, Buddhism, Jainism and Sikhism. Much like *nirvana*, *moksha* means to be free of the cycle of death and rebirth due to the principle of *karma* (another word that is said to be impossible to translate). *Moksha* could be translated as 'freedom' or 'liberation', but neither is adequate: *moksha* is *moksha*; it arises and relates to a particular world view.

Untranslated terms are not always from living languages. The Italian philosopher Giorgio Agamben's influential book *Homo Sacer: Sovereign Power and Bare Life* (1998, first published in 1995 as *Homo sacer: Il potere sovrano e la nuda vita*) stacks up three claims to originality by making use of two 'new words' ('sovereign power' and 'bare life')[9] and fronting them with the obscure Latin expression *Homo Sacer* ('sacred man'; a Roman legal category for someone who can be killed by anyone and has no civic rights).[10] Agamben reanimates this ancient category and ties it to his two neologisms to argue that the art of statecraft and politics relies on demarcating certain lives as without legal worth.

How to work with international words

Taking an interest in translation will help most students who want to push their topics in innovative directions. You can add original value to existing terms or create your own (perhaps drawing on your own language skills). Where an untranslated term is clear and prominent in your area of study, you can show originality by engaging it in one or both of the two ways identified below.

Note: Where students find no such terms in their reading lists or lectures (and this is not uncommon in the more monoglot parts of the English-speaking world), the second method is still applicable, as it addresses how topics can be misunderstood through mistranslation.

1. *Explore and engage a relatively new international word that is current in your area of study.* In some disciplines and courses, especially those with international reach, such terms are plentiful. However, students need to make sure they are 'adding to' them in a substantive and original way. You can do this by engaging untranslated words with the kind of original themes discussed in Chapter 2 and using the techniques discussed earlier in this chapter.

Sample sentences:

In this essay the new political power of Hindutva ideology will be framed in terms of Agamben's theory of 'bare life'.

Note: Here a well-known term for an Indian political ideology – Hindutva – is brought into conversation with a well-known theory. The originality does not reside in either one but in their being brought together.

This essay draws on the work of Yellow and Red to reimagine and revisit the situationist notion of *détournement* through a post-colonial lens.

Note: Here is another example of originality stemming from a 'bringing together'. In this case, it is supported by an explicit claim to be giving new life ('reimagine' and 'revisit') to an avant-garde practice first developed in 1950s France, *détournement* (a diversion, or turning about).

2. *Explore the context of translation and/or critique a translation.* It is often the case that terms are imported from other languages without consideration for either the context in which they arose or the possibility of other translations. Exploring either of these areas can provide an original intervention.

Samples sentences:

The study of *apartheid* South Africa has tended to neglect the historical origins of the term in Afrikaans' mythology and cultural history. Often associated with the period 1948–1992, this essay draws on recent studies by Blue and Red to arrive at a longer historical perspective on the ideology of *apartheid*.

Note: Here the Afrikaans word *apartheid* – meaning 'held apart' – is used as the centrepiece of a re-examination of South African history. The approach is anchored by reference to academic authorities.

The perception and reception of the work of the Gutai art group has been shaped by the translation of their work for a Western audience, specifically the translation of *gutai* as 'embodiment' or 'concrete'. In this essay, I draw on the work of Pink to show that the term '*gutai*' was designed to signal a rejection of European avant-gardes and both abstract and figurative art.

Note: Here the Japanese name of a Japanese art movement is used as a launching point for an essay on its interpretation and intentions.

My references in the two sentences above are made up. Let's look at a real example. It can be argued that understanding Sigmund Freud's 'new words' (and there are many; we already saw one, *unheimlich*, and another example is *narzissmus* or 'narcissism') requires an understanding of the context of their birth, in late nineteenth-century Vienna. Even more striking, in the case of Freud, is the nature of the translations applied to some of his 'new words'.[11] These translations profoundly altered how Freud was understood internationally. For example, his trio *Ich* (directly translated: 'I'), *Es* ('it') and *Uber-Ich* ('over-I') was translated into English, and other languages, via Latin, so becoming the more expansive and suggestive 'ego', 'id' and 'superego'.

Here is another example, this time from the study of 'race' and 'ethnicity' in China. Placing those words in inverted commas shows that I have them under surveillance. These words are often used in Western-language debates about China, but are they appropriate? Do they mislead us? Have people in China now or in the past thought of people, inside or outside their country, as being divided by 'race'? In English, the term implies communities with clear inherited physical differences. Some scholars argue that there is a long history of race-thinking in China.[12] This argument relies, in part, on translating the Chinese words *zu* and *minzu* as 'race'. If you do that, you can find Chinese writings about 'race' going back centuries. Others are doubtful. They argue that the idea of race in China is a Western import and that these Chinese terms do not refer to physically distinct peoples. Thus, for example, the word 'zu', it has been argued, refers to established, historical separate communities; not 'race' as someone in the West might understand 'race'.[13]

This is a very specific example and you might think it sounds too specialised and particular to emulate. But pause a moment: that reaction tells us something. It tells us that, with a little effort and care, exploring how a word is translated goes a long way; it has scholarly weight and it impresses. Perhaps you can think of a word that is important to your topic or subject area and do some preliminary research about how it is transposed to other societies, with different traditions and languages. Typing 'translation' and 'language' along with other key terms into an academic search engine may direct you to an existing literature that can anchor your work.

TIP

Using the word 'foreign'

In multicultural and multilingual societies, calling languages that are widely spoken 'foreign' can be inappropriate. The term 'foreign languages' may be replaced by 'global languages' or 'international languages' and 'foreign word' by, for example, 'non-English word'.

TRY THIS

Aim: To explore key words through translation

Sometimes untranslated terms are obvious in the titles of papers and books on your reading list. If so, *try this*: limiting your search to the last 10 years, type 'critique' (or a similar word) and the most common of these untranslated words into a search engine. What you are looking for are attempts to develop and re-examine this key term. You may also find an anchor text that does something similar and provides a launching point for your own engagement.

At other times, untranslated terms are hard to find. If so, *try this*: take a key word from your area of study and explore its meaning and usage in another language. It does not need to be a 'new word'. In fact, this exercise works better if it is a well-known word. Earlier I looked at the way the English word 'race' translates into Chinese as my example. Here's an illustration between more similar languages. To adapt it for your own use all you need to do is replace the key term and the language. This illustration is of a translation that might seem not to change much. The key term is 'geopolitics' and the language is Italian. 'Geopolitics' translates into Italian as *geopolitica* (with the same meaning but a somewhat different heritage and debate). Type this Italian term in an academic search engine, time-limiting your search. A lot of Italian commentary on *geopolitica* will come up. If you can read Italian so much the better; if not, do what I do and use a translate function to look at one or two essays. What you are looking for is either a sense of the distinctive context and heritage of the Italian debate or evidence of an original contemporary Italian debate, or 'take', on geopolitics. Here is one example of the kind of sentence that may emerge from this evidence: 'In this essay English-language geopolitics are reframed through an encounter with the specific concerns of Italian debates on *geopolitica.*'

Inventing your own words

Inventing your own new words is not as daunting as it may appear. Here are two ways to do it:

1. *Adding to existing labels.* In other words, creating what I have called 'composite' terms. This is the approach I recommend. It is straightforward and less risky than method 2 (creating your own neologism). Say, for example, you want to talk about hospitals in a sociology course. 'This essay outlines "hospital sociology" as a distinct societal arena…'. Studying horses in geography? 'I develop and identify the field of "equine geography" as a contribution to the new sub-field of "animal geographies"'. As the last example hints, there is a limit to how niche you can go: more minor topics are best slotted into existing sub-fields. Here are some more examples. Interested in exploring South

Asian material in a course on memory? Why not argue that 'South Asian Memory Studies' should be recognised as a distinctive area of enquiry? Want to engage the work of specific Feminist Marxist authors with post-colonialism? You are off to a good start: being specific in at least one of these areas is a lot more likely to lead to originality than working with very broad traditions (if your ambition was to 'engage the work of Marxists', it would sound too general). Next step, come up with a category. For example, perhaps you could write 'this is a body of work that can be grouped under the label "post-race Feminist Marxism"'. You are looking for just one word to combine with the existing label: 'new words' lose effect if strung into long phrases, so try to keep your constructions short and punchy.

As this last case tells us, you can also take inspiration from the academic penchant for finding and categorising 'posts' (and 'beyonds' and 'afters'). You will need to make sure that the work or phenomenon you are describing does indeed critique and/or signal a departure from whatever you are claiming it is 'post' to. It bears repeating that having one substantial innovation is better than trying, and probably failing, to introduce several. So, for example, keep to one 'post' and get it upfront, anchored and clear. For example: 'In this essay, I draw on the work of Blue in order to identify a new phenomenon in public architecture, which I call the "post-civic"'. Such a sentence is focused and specific, and promises something ambitious but doable.

2. *Inventing your own neologism.* For students, creating your own new word from scratch presents more of a risk than adding to an existing one. My advice is don't. There is a chance that such terms will sound redundant, unwanted, even a bit silly. I'm playing safe. Too safe maybe. Let's say you want to give it a go.

There are many ways to create single new words but the simplest form is another type of composite. 'Mythogeography', 'schizocartography', 'sostalgia' are three examples of new words that all take an existing root ('geography', 'cartography', 'algia') and splice it with another term. If it suddenly feels like we have wandered into a Greek or Latin class, that is because Greek (ancient not modern) and Latin are the privileged languages for this kind of operation. There is no reason why you can't do it with other languages, but these ones remain the most widely used. 'Algia' is Greek for pain and sickness. We know it from its combination with the Greek for 'homecoming' (*nostos*); creating 'nostalgia' or home sickness (a word that was invented in the late seventeenth century). 'Sostalgia' splices the Latin root for 'comfort' – *solacium* – into 'algia', creating a neolgism which today is sometimes used to describe a sense of loss in the face of environmental change. It is an instructive example, for there is nothing in either of the contributing root words directly about the environment. So long as the author's definition is in the same ball-park as the literal meaning that is fine; the inventor is the one who defines the invention.

Let's give it a go. I'll also start with 'algia' (sickness), as it is a common root word and widely understood. Let's create a brand new composite with it. The Latin for night is *nyx*. So *nyxalgia* literally means 'night sick-ness'. To make this new word work for us we will want to define it less literally. For example, we could define it as referring to modern societies' fear of the dark. In summary, the 'word-creating' process has three stages: identify a root, find a word or word-part to combine with it, and then define the word's meaning.

TRY THIS

Aim: Devise your own new word

This exercise is based on your last written assignment. Could its argument have been improved and made more original if you had devised a 'new word'? Stick to adding to an existing label, as this is the most common and practical option. Can you see a group of scholars, or type of scholarship, which could be given a particular label, one based on adding a word to a pre-existing sub-field or topic field? It is important that you don't force the point. Realising that, no, such a term would be unhelpful, because it would corral people and things together that don't have a clear connection, is more useful than imposing a label that doesn't fit. In fact, it is one successful outcome of the exercise. What you are aiming at is not a list of 'new words', come what may, but to start to think about when and why innovative categorisations work and when they don't.

Conclusion

Words matter. One way of reading this chapter is as a supplement to Chapter 2. There we explored six types of original argument. The new words and phrases introduced in this chapter can help communicate any of these six arguments. However, to restrict an interest in language to a supplementary role is to miss the centrality of language in innova-tion. As we have seen, there are many cases where discussion of how and why certain terms are used is at the heart of pioneering work. In part, this centrality reflects the mutable nature of language. Language is constantly being adapted and diversified to accommodate social change and the agendas of different groups. It is a peculiarly plastic thing that can be shaped and reshaped by many different actors.

Academic language tries to capture this mobility and its formal, precise and often rather laborious nature provides both a structure and a tradition through which the world can be dissected and understood. It is, however, worth thinking about how this distinctive academic dialect frames the world. Critics often accuse academics of writing in impenetrable prose and of being more concerned with communicating with a tiny community of colleagues than with the public. There is tolerance for mathematicians and physicists to express themselves in terms that take years to master but, understandably, far less leeway is given to scholars in the humanities or social sciences. It is useful to acknowledge such concerns for they reflect the rising importance across higher education of a commitment to impact and dissemination (both of which provide many opportunities for student innovation, as discussed in Chapter 6). These topics also force us to face a wider question: 'What is academic language trying to achieve?' My answer is that it is attempting, or should be attempting, to depict and understand reality in all its complexity without sacrificing clarity. This fundamental ambition, to be both truthful and lucid, is always worth bearing in mind, especially for students on the pathway to originality.

4

Original Methods

Introduction

Every essay, every talk, everything you do, has a method. Yet methodology often goes undiscussed and follows a formula: you do what everyone has done before. In your field, people usually pick out some quotes and write about them, so you do that; or they analyse a raft of statistics, so you do that. This conservatism makes method fertile territory for those who want to break free and do something new. It also disguises the fact that methodological originality is all the rage. Recent years have seen a huge leap forward in the range of methods used by academics. For students, what this means is that even being modestly innovative with your methods is likely to be well received and can lift your assignment to a new level.

This chapter has four parts. The first is about making your methods more original. It follows the pattern seen throughout this book: you take the innovation of a named authority figure – 'drawing on the work of...' – and in some way develop or add to it. In all assessment types, it is advisable to anchor any innovative treatment of methods in the academic literature. The second part is about critiquing other people's methods in an original fashion. This process often involves identifying, and thus 'making visible', these methods. These two parts and these two approaches are not an either/or choice: you can do both, i.e., creating 'your own' method can flow directly from critiquing an existing method.

Since it is sometimes hard to think what other methods are available to you, in the third section I provide a short list. I doubt this itemisation contains even 1 per cent of the methods you could choose. It is not designed to be exhaustive but merely to open up the topic as one of argument and choice. In the fourth and last part, I look at how originality in methods can work in different types of assignment. There is an assumption in many quarters that only the long, final-year, research-led essay – the 10,000-word dissertation, for example – provides room for explicit discussion of method, and thus methodological innovation. This is not true. Everything you do has a method and most types of assignment can benefit from methodological innovation.

TIP

Methods need to suit the mission

Methodological innovation should flow from your task and your topic. You innovate because your task or topic benefits from it. Methods have to suit the mission. Originality that has no rhyme or reason, and appears to be there for its own sake, detracts from an assignment and may lose you marks.

Three ways of making your methods original

There are many ways to make your methods original. I introduce three of the most reliable methods. The first is about *engaging innovation in your own field*, i.e., scoping your topic or discipline, identifying a methodological innovation, and then, in some way, developing it. The second involves being innovative by *bringing in a method from another area of study* (another discipline, for example), and the third points to originality achieved by using a *mixture of methods*.

Engaging with innovation in your field

In most disciplines, longer journal papers and most research monographs give some, and sometimes lengthy and explicit, attention to methodology. Even so, scoping for methodological innovation can be daunting. You need to identify and engage an existing innovation but one that is relatively recent, such as from the last decade or so. The more open-ended this search is the longer it will take. It saves time if you already know the kind of method that interests you. Alternatively, using an academic search engine, you can add search terms such as 'innovative method', 'new method', 'original method', or similar, to a specific topic and hope to come across a promising paper or book. With a little persistence, this kind of academic free diving can lead you to pearls. You then have to decide which, if any, of your finds you want to take home.

Here are three case studies of this process in action. Remember that, by preference, you should be 'drawing from' and 'adding to' work that is not too old (for example, work published in the last 10 years – remember, this range is just a rough guide; it can be more).

CASE STUDY I

Discipline: Business Studies

Innovation: A. Alexandra Michel's (2007) use of 'insider experience' to study behaviour and attitude change in investment banking.

In this passage, Michel (2007) tells us why her innovative method made a difference:

> My personal experience increased my empathy with informants and positioned me as an in-group member, such that bankers included me in work and sometimes non-work activities and trusted me with private information. Both empathy and social inclusion were crucial for investigating cognitive change processes.[1]

Michel makes it clear that an 'insider' approach is pioneering in her field and she anchors this innovation by reference to ethnographic studies in sociology. One way you could develop and engage this idea is by expanding the implications of 'insider experience':

> *Sample sentence*: Drawing on Michel's innovative use of 'insider experience' to gain access to her subjects, I show how my own experiences in the business community both enabled and hindered my access to the field.

Note: This is not a mere repetition of Michel but builds on her work by suggesting that 'insider' experience can cut both ways when it comes to access.

CASE STUDY II

Discipline: English Literature

Innovation: Michael Stubbs' (2005) use of a quantitative method ('corpus stylistics') to study literary texts.

(Continued)

Stubbs' (2005) innovation was to apply and defend quantitative techniques, such as enumerating key words and cognates, in the study of literary texts. He explains that '[s]tylistics has long led an uneasy half-life, never fully accepted, for many related reasons, by either linguists or literary critics', and goes on to argue:

> The findings of corpus stylistics (comparative frequencies, distributions and the like) sometimes document more systematically what literary critics already know (and therefore add to methods of close reading), but they can also reveal otherwise invisible features of long texts.[2]

Stubbs makes it clear that a quantitative approach remains marginal within the wider discipline (and notes a number of fierce critics) but also that it has a particular contribution to make. One straightforward way of developing and engaging with this innovation is to argue that this claimed methodological stand-off could be overcome.

> *Sample sentence*: Although quantitative and qualitative methods in stylistic analysis have been framed as a schism (Stubbs), in this essay I draw on both and show how each throws different but equally valuable light on the interpretation of [specific text].

Note: This is not merely a 'both sides are right' argument, which can appear like fence-sitting, but a clear claim on the utility of mixing both methods.

CASE STUDY III

Discipline: Education

Innovation: The use of material objects when conducting interviews with children.

Jennifer Rowsell's (2011) interviews with 11–14-year-old learners from African-American and Caribbean-American backgrounds were enabled and framed by her request that they bring in and talk about personal objects that they valued.

> Artifacts and the study of artifacts as a methodology have become an area of inquiry for theorists across different fields. ... The bracelet, the ribbon, the jersey, the necklace provided fractures of each learner that open up worlds that we can use as educators to make greater meaning and relevance to our teaching and learning of English (particularly

for students who feel marginalized). Getting to know students and see how they crossed from a classroom space into a more personal space by talking about objects that they love gave me more of an aperture to analyze their pathway into writing.[3]

Rowsell sets her approach within a wider turn towards using artifacts to elicit information. As this suggests, her innovation centres on bringing an emerging, interdisciplinary approach to bear on young learners. To engage her contribution, requires that we specify it and indicate how it can be developed. For a student in education studies, a sample sentence that does this might be:

Sample sentence: Drawing on Rowsell's use of a material objects methodology to 'open up' young people's attitudes to learning and, more specifically, the attitudes of 'students who feel marginalised', this essay will argue that a similar approach can be of use when working with students who are deaf.

TIP

Team and solo work

There is a big difference between the methods available to lone researchers (which often includes students) and people working in a team. Research methods that rely on a team of researchers cannot be fully replicated by an individual. If you do want to make use of – to engage and develop – a method drawn from the work of a research team, you will need to adapt it. What this means is that you need to acknowledge the team nature of the study you are drawing from, and that you trim and refine it in a way that makes sense for a lone scholar.

Bringing in a method from another area of study

All the case studies I introduced above were doing something that is often at the heart of fresh methodological thinking: importing a technique from another area of study. Michel took from sociology, specifically ethnomethodology, Stubbs from what he calls 'computational' or 'computer-assisted' approaches, and Rowsell from the new interdisciplinary field of material studies. You can do the same. This process is very common in academic writing but – a word of warning – it only works when the imported methodology is a good fit, i.e., if it responds to clearly identified methodological challenges. Justifying your choice of import is crucial. This can be assisted if you anchor your choice in the work of an academic author or authors in your discipline who have recently done the same. Let's look at two more case studies to see this in action.

CASE STUDY I

Discipline: Community Psychology

Innovation: Caterina Arcidiacono et al. (2016) bring 'visual methods' into their field and combine them with 'participatory action research' (which is already well established in community psychology).

Arcidiacono et al. (2016) explain this import as follows:

> the display and sharing of the content of visual materials has the main goal of opening up new communication channels between researchers, local actors, stakeholders and local authorities. This, in turn, leads to a shared dialogue and debate, which is key to the exchange of views and the search for possible solutions to local problems.[4]

> *Sample sentence*: Drawing on Arcidiacono et al.'s introduction of visual methods into community psychology, this study proposes a new critical visual approach, in which visual materials are both co-produced and co-critiqued by researcher and researcher.

Note: Here the new method is adopted but also adapted; a move that is flagged by claiming a 'new critical' take on visual methods.

CASE STUDY II

Discipline: Indigenous Studies

Innovation: Arts-based approaches.

Recent years have witnessed arts-based research methods applied in 'indigenous studies'. A rationale for this import is offered by Hammond et al. (2018) in an article that scopes a range of research projects that use arts-based methods. They argue that '[n]ew "indigenizing" methodologies centre the production of knowledge around the processes and knowledges of indigenous communities', and conclude that creative research methods 'involving artistic practices—such as photovoice, journaling, digital storytelling, dance, and theatre—may have a place within these new approaches'.[5]

Sample sentence: The recent development of 'arts-based' and 'co-production' methodologies in studies by and about indigenous peoples remains geographically limited to the study of the indigenous experience in 'settler societies'. In this study we apply and develop this method in the context of the indigenous experience in South East Asia.

Note: This is an example of a geographical shift creating originality (see Chapter 2).

TRY THIS

Aim: To identify an existing methodological innovation related to your assignment topic and think of one or two ways you can develop it

Type in search terms as specific and close as possible to your assignment topic and add 'methods', 'methodology', or related terms, such as 'research approach', 'qualitative', 'quantitative'. Limit your search to the past 10 years or so. If you are able to locate a list of possible articles, note down in as few words as possible the methodological innovations that interest you. Try to put a very brief – one- or two-word – label on these innovations. What are they called? What will you call them? Next, working with just one of these innovations, note down one or two ways you can engage and add to it. This can be simple reorientation – a geographical shift, for example – or it can include the use of a 'new word' prefix ('critical', 'reflexive', 'post-', and so on).

Mixing methods as innovation

Diversity is often a source of innovation. One way of anchoring a diverse approach is by pitching your work as embracing 'mixed methods' and/or 'methodological pluralism'. This approach can draw from the extensive literature on 'mixed methods' (which even has its own journals, such as *Journal of Mixed Methods Research*). Many of these studies argue for combining quantitative and qualitative approaches. However, the more specific the ingredients and purpose of your 'mixture' the better. Without this kind of specificity, simply claiming to be adopting 'mixed methods' is likely to appear too general and, since it has a considerable pedigree in many disciplines, will not be seen as innovative.

CASE STUDY

Discipline: Ethnography/Media Studies

Innovation: Mixing qualitative, quantitative and multimodal social media data.

Roser Beneito-Montagut (2011) analysed and enumerated interactions on MySpace, Twitter and Facebook.[6] She also interviewed six internet users and captured screenshots and saved hyperlinks. Her approach was mixed and multimodal, designed specifically to capture the complexity and range of internet usage.

Sample sentence: Drawing on the innovative mixed methods pioneered by Beneito-Montagut, this essay argues that the complexity of online interactions receives insufficient attention in the wider field of social media research.

Critiquing method

Critiquing someone's methods can offer powerful insight, but your critique needs to be substantial, not based on a minor detail, but on challenging something basic. One approach is to identify the dominant type of method in an area and to question this dominance. This type of argument often concludes that this dominance is limiting and distorting research outcomes. Both of the case studies I introduce below show this, but they also buck the advice I have been giving to be specific, as each concerns general claims about quantitative methods. Although this can be taken to indicate that general critiques can occasionally be useful, for students, these two examples show how general critiques can act as jumping off points for something that is usually more suitable, which is to offer more particular interventions and challenges (as shown in the sample sentences).

CASE STUDY I

Discipline: History of sociology

Innovation: Challenging the dominance of qualitative methods.

Geoff Payne (2014) has critiqued what he calls the 'myth' that sociology was once dominated by quantitative and 'positivist' methods. This 'myth' he says is put to work to sanction and reproduce the dominance of qualitative approaches among 'non-numerate' scholars. He says:

> the myth of sociology's quantitative/'positivist' past ... [is] invoked to protect the self-interest of ... generations of non-numerate sociologists.[7]

> *Sample sentence*: Drawing on Payne's challenge to what he calls the 'myth' of sociology's positivist heritage, this essay argues that the discipline's social justice agenda has been compromised by its inability to verify and evidence its arguments.

CASE STUDY II

Discipline: Organisational psychology

Innovation: Critiquing the quantitative paradigm.

Symon et al. (2000) challenge the dominance of quantitative methods in organisational psychology and offer an alternative framework:

> we argue that work and organizational psychology is still dominated by quantitative research studies based on positivist beliefs about the conduct of research. Drawing on Symon and Cassell (1999), we suggest a number of reasons for this continuing situation. ... We conclude by recommending the consideration of alternative approaches and practices to European [work and organisational] psychologists.[8]

> *Sample sentence*: Drawing on Symon et al.'s challenge to the dominance of quantitative methods in organisational psychology, this essay shows the utility of a visual and arts-based method.

Note: Symon et al. 'draw on' the work of their own team of authors. This kind of self-citation is an indication that they are making a claim to be the first to make this argument.

TRY THIS

Aim: Critique a methodological innovation

Identify a methodological innovation in your field and/or related to your topic. Write down three ways this innovation could be challenged. You may wish to think about the following questions:

- Is it limited in its sources or application?
- Does it misrepresent the traditions it seeks to depart from?
- Is it simplistic, either in terms of practice or its likely outcome?

From this list identify one that seems the strongest, most robust critique. This will be substantive sounding, the one that is likely to be seen as contributing the most value to methodological debate.

Methods: An incomplete list

What is fresh in one field may be tired in another. The challenge is to work out what is innovative in respect of your particular field and for your particular assignment. To do so you need to scope your field and topic and to have a sense of the range of methodological choices that researchers can make. Below I present a *very limited* list of some of the more general traditions. There are thousands of methods, so the fact that I have likely not included a method you know of or intend to use is neither a problem nor surprising. The following list should be understood as an initial exercise in thinking about the *variety* of methods at our disposal.

The examples I provide below are starting points, not destinations. Remember: we have already seen that it is often better to engage and develop particular methods. For example, one of the sample sentences introduced earlier made the case for a 'new critical visual approach' and specified this 'new' and 'critical' aspect as stemming from the way the method was 'co-produced and co-critiqued'. The broader the methodological tradition, the more it needs finessing, particularising and anchoring.

Qualitative and quantitative methods represent important orientations of research, so I gather most of my examples under these headings. However, it is important to note that this distinction reflects traditional attributions rather than logical demarcations. All the 'qualitative methods' below *could* be quantitative (and that might be an original approach to take to them). Moreover, in practice, a lot of research mixes the qualitative and quantitative, so I conclude my list with various 'mixed methods'.

Qualitative: refers to the collection of non-numerical data and the application of non-statistical techniques.

Archive: searching for and extracting information and evidence from official and unofficial archives.

Documentary: the use of official or personal documents as a source of information. These can include policy documents, diaries, web pages, novels, court transcripts and ephemera such as leaflets and tweets.

Interviews: these can be with individuals or groups; they can happen once or take place over years; they can take place in many different settings (from the most formal to the 'on the go' walking interview); they can be structured, semi-structured or unstructured.

Textual: understanding the language, symbols and/or pictures present in texts to gain information. This tradition overlaps with many other traditions, such as the analysis of discourse (patterns of speech and communication), narrative analysis (which focuses on stories) and conversation analysis (which addresses both the non-verbal and the verbal content of everyday interaction).

Reflexive: relating method to aspects of one's personal or social biography, often, but not always, in order to interrogate the nature of one's access to and understanding of power and knowledge.

Visual: comprising a collection of methods that incorporate visual elements, such as maps, drawings, photographs and videos, as well as three-dimensional objects into the research process. It also includes techniques such as photo-elicitation, photovoice, draw-and-write and cognitive mapping. Innovation in visual methods is not only about choice of technique, but also about issues of how they are used and by whom.

Material: uses objects (for example, personal possessions) as interview prompts, as sites of discussion and as storied forms.

Biographical: based on an account of a person's or institution's life, a biographical method can establish relationships between initial events and their outcomes. When focused on people, this approach can overlap with phenomenological methods, which address participants' perceptions and understanding of their experiences.

Oral: usually framed as oral history, a method of conducting historical research through recorded interview with a narrator who has personal experience of a period, place or events.

Feminist/Anti-racist: interrogates the limits of traditional methodologies to capture the gendered/racialised nature of knowledge and experience. It offers alternative, emancipatory and critical techniques and approaches.

Community-based: a range of collaborative approaches have been devised, including Critical Communicative Methodology (which has an emphasis on the critical capacities of participants) and Participatory Action Research (a form of collaborative and community research with a focus on social change and community empowerment). It also overlaps with 'co-produced' methods, in which participants work together on an agreed topic without privileging scholar over subject.

Quantitative: refers to the collection of numerical data and the application of statistical techniques.

Data visualisation: the graphical representation of data. By using visual elements such as charts, graphs and maps, data visualisation tools provide an accessible way to see and understand trends, outliers and patterns in data.

Sampling: for large data forms, sampling is used for analysis. Various forms of sampling exist, including random, convenience, systematic, cluster and stratified. The representativeness of a population may be assessed and related to a sample size.

Descriptive statistics: describes the relationship between variables in a sample or population. Descriptive statistics provide a summary of data in the form of mean, median, mode and associated range and variance.

Inferential statistics: uses a sample of data taken from a population to describe and make inferences about the whole population (using measures of probability and correlation). It is valuable when it is not possible to examine each member of an entire population.

Mixed methods: in practice, a lot of research mixes quantitative and qualitative research, and this act of combination can itself be a source of innovation, especially in respect of topics or disciplines that favour one approach over the other.

Content analysis: a systematic, enumerating approach to analysing the nature and meaning of texts and forms of communication.

Longitudinal: observation-based, and often correlation-based, study that involves monitoring a population over an extended period of time.

Questionnaires and surveys: can produce both qualitative or quantitative data which can then be analysed separately or together.

Critical quantitative research methods: use of quantitative methods in alignment with social justice methods, such as anti-racism and feminism.

Innovative methods for different types of written assessment

Dissertations

Because of its length and because it often allows students to do their own research, the dissertation can sometimes appear the only type of assignment that provides explicit encouragement to innovate on methods. What this tells us is not that methodology should not be addressed in other assignments, but that paying attention to methods, and thus thinking about how to be original with one's methods, is usually a key part of an outstanding dissertation. Even when you have already worked on the originality of your overall argument and topic, the dissertation provides the scope to contribute an innovative approach to your methods. It also provides an opportunity to engage with issues of dissemination and impact (see Chapter 6). This innovation should be clearly signposted. It needs to be flagged in the overall Introduction and Conclusion to the dissertation and, most importantly, in the opening paragraphs of the section or chapter in which you discuss your methodology.

Examinations

Unless the examination assignment is specifically about methods, there is a tendency for students not to consider the topic of methods in exam responses and for examiners not to expect them to be discussed. This provides an opportunity for students to do something that stands out. As long as you anchor your contribution in an academic source, foregrounding an argument about methods as your main argument or adding an argument about methods as supplementary to your principal argument can show both breadth of reading and innovation.

Essays

As with examinations, an inventive methodological intervention can often be an unexpected, and thus distinctive, thing to do when writing an essay. As with exams, foregrounding an argument about methods as your main argument or adding an argument about methods as supplementary to your principal argument can be equally effective. Within essays, it is useful to provide a range of source references, especially for your anchor authors. Showing an awareness that the application of a methodology by a named authority varies, for example by being developed or expanded between two examples of their work, exhibits acuteness and depth of reading.

Conclusions: Don't be put off

Despite being a required criterion for receiving the best marks, the academic world continues to treat originality – perhaps, especially, methodological originality – as almost out of reach. An overview of methodological originality in Business Studies by Lê and Schmid (2022) concludes that the 'process of innovating research methods entails advanced expert knowledge and skill'.[9] It is a forbidding message. Yet on further examination, we see that Lê and Schmid's sombre warning does *not* mean that students cannot be methodologically original. It reflects something else: that academic staff research and student research are different animals. All of Lê and Schmid's examples of innovation involve teams of researchers, spread over several countries, doing work over several years and gathering large amounts of data. A lot of academic work has at least one of these characteristics: lots of people and a range of issues concerning access and coordination. No wonder they think it requires 'advanced' and 'expert' levels of ability. These conditions do not apply to student work. That doesn't make student work any less capable of originality, but it does make it different. Student assignments are very time-limited, and are often done alone or in small teams of fellow students. Their claim to methodological originality will, of course, be simpler and more likely focused on one innovation. That is the nature of the beast: it is not lesser, just different, and it is definitely within reach.

5

Creative Practice

Introduction

There are two parts to this chapter. In the first, I show how students in non-arts-based disciplines can make use of arts-based techniques to transform their work. The second part is directed to students in the 'creative disciplines', which include fine art, performance, graphics, fashion and creative writing.

This divide is not as clear as it used to be. Today many students in, for example, psychology or English can choose modules with creative practice content. At the same time, many arts-based disciplines have taken a social and political turn, so they are increasingly outward-looking and interdisciplinary.

Creativity is the ability to impress a distinct, innovative and expressive vision upon an outcome. Arts-based disciplines are understood to be the epitome of this process, and are therefore identified with creative practice. This identification also means that people often assume that the 'creative disciplines' are where originality finds its true home. This assumption is understandable but wrong. As we shall see, whether you are making a film, painting a canvas or writing an essay about ancient Egyptian field-rotation, the types of originality that will work for you take the same form: they all involve linking, adding to and critically engaging traditions and existing innovations.

Arts-based practice: A student's guide

What is arts-based practice?

Arts-based practice incorporates techniques, processes and outcomes derived from the creative disciplines to improve presentation and aid research and its dissemination. As the term implies, arts-based *practice* refers to *doing* something creative. Discussing a short story is not arts-based practice; writing one – or getting one's research subjects to write one – is. The first two decades of the twenty-first century witnessed a remarkable rise and expansion of arts-based practice in many areas. The most common forms it has taken are: drama, photography, fiction (stories and poems), non-fiction (narratives, autobiographies and diaries), painting, sculpture, comics, maps, music, film, and diverse online and virtual recordings and events.

There are three types of arts-based practice. All three can be used together or in any combination:

1. *As an aesthetic contribution.* Art forms can be used to enrich otherwise conventional work. One minor but well-used example is the epigraph, a quote set at the beginning of a chapter or at the start of a section, often taken from a novel or poem. Another is the use of photographs, or other images, that illustrate a topic but also contribute an aesthetic dimension. Both of these aesthetic contributions are a relatively safe choice for students, and they can lift the look (and nudge the mark) of an assignment and help its claim to originality. Although they may appear superficial, these interventions are often judged to be innovative, in large part because, in many disciplines, so few students bother with them. 'Presentation' is a common, and commonly overlooked, assessment criterion; and even when it is not, it still makes a difference. However, don't go overboard. It is important that such 'aesthetic contributions' are targeted and thoughtful. They need to be directly relevant to one's topic and must not appear arbitrary or excessive. Sprinkling unexplained images through an essay is likely to detract from your mark. As with other figures, all images need to be properly referenced, captioned and explained in the text. For more on illustrations and other things you can do with text, see the section 'Style and form' in this chapter.

2. *As part of the research process.* Art-based techniques are used to conduct and assist research, for example by eliciting research information. One common example is asking one's research subjects to take photographs or make drawings and then to get them to talk through their images and choices. It has been argued that this process is particularly useful when trying to elicit information from groups who are 'hard-to-reach', such as people who are socially vulnerable and children. More generally, arts-based work is often concerned with giving agency to the disempowered, thus the title of one commentary, 'Arts-based inquiry: the natural partner for social justice'.[1]

3. *Art as outcome.* This outcome can take many forms, such as an exhibition of gathered objects, texts or interviewees' work, a website featuring photographs, or a performance that re-enacts the lives of subjects through their own words.

Students' use of arts-based practice is framed by the assignment criteria they are given and the timeframes they have to work with. In *exams*, it is rarely possible to use arts-based practice. In *essays*, it is possible to use art as an 'aesthetic contribution' but, outside those increasing number of courses where it is required or encouraged, there may be little room to develop it as a research process. By contrast, in many but not all disciplines, *dissertations* provide considerable scope for the first two forms of arts-based practice identified above. The third form is something of a stretch, given the constraints on student time, but should be borne in mind. Arts-based practice can also be used in *presentations* (see Chapter 6). In summary, for most student essays, option 1 is straightforward and option 2 is sometimes doable, especially in longer, research-based work, while option 3 is often out of reach but worth thinking about.

Who creates?

There is a 'researcher-as-creator' to 'subject-as-creator' continuum. At one end, art is produced solely by the researcher, and at the other end, it is produced solely by those who are being researched. Traditionally, the art produced in the 'creative disciplines' has been at the former terminus of this line, while most arts-based work in other disciplines has been more towards the other end and is said to be 'co-produced' and 'co-created'. This zone on the continuum is also where one hears diverse political claims about art as 'giving voice' and as a form of 'empowerment'. In an essay on how to use cinema and video in research, Anne Harris (2018) throws out the following questions to would-be practitioners:

> Are you using video to include others in your research who might normally be marginalized or backgrounded in 'scholarly work'? Are you using it to hand over or share power and control of your research project? Are you using it to foreground your own voice or that of others who are normally sidelined or silenced in a global forum or an academic context?[2]

Can I incorporate arts-based research in my discipline?

The use of arts-based practice in the research process is uneven between disciplines. It is widely accepted in parts of psychology, and not uncommon in anthropology and education studies, but it remains marginal in most fields within history. In between, there is a range of disciplines, such as geography and business studies, where arts-based work is a new trend that is increasingly welcomed but remains peripheral to the mainstream. What this means for students is that their use of arts-based practice will be judged, in large part, by if and how it has been adopted in their discipline. The result is a balancing act. In those fields, such as some sub-fields within psychology, where arts-based work is a well-trodden path, students can be confident that it is acceptable, but they will have to work hard to 'add value' – to 'work with' existing traditions – in order to appear original. In other disciplines, by contrast, arts-based interventions are likely to appear intrinsically original but students *may* have to work hard to show their academic value and overcome resistance.

In an overview of the use of arts-based practice in psychology, anthropology and sociology, Jessica Smartt Gullion and Lisa Schäfer (2018) conclude that:

> Psychologists have much more readily embraced [arts-based research] and practices than their counterparts. ... This is particularly true in the areas of counselling, clinical psychology, and educational psychology.[3]

This overview reinforces the point that some disciplines are more receptive than others, but, more specifically, so are some sub-fields. What may be considered fine for students in educational psychology may not to be so well received in neuropsychology.

TIP

Always anchor your use of arts-based methods in the academic literature and establish how your use is engaging previous studies

This is important both in disciplines and sub-disciplines with established traditions of using arts-based work and in disciplines where it is a slender current. In both cases you have to show that you understand and are building on existing practice. In the case of disciplines or sub-disciplines where arts-based work is undeveloped, any student who wants to make use of it needs to tread carefully (also see below: 'Arts-based practice: Critical questions'). Your arts-based practice needs to be justified and explained. This can be done by anchoring it in the few examples that may exist (there is usually at least one) or, failing that, you can anchor it in calls found in the academic literature for 'more creative' approaches. If you are unsure how your use of art-based practice will be received, you must check with your tutor or course leader. The more specific you can be about what you intend to do the more helpful this conversation will be.

Style and form

There are many ways of writing. You can be personal or dry, you can opt for the usual format that has always worked for you (for example, Introduction plus two/three sub-headings plus Conclusion) or do something different. But let's be honest, most of all, you have to do what you are told. Students are not free agents. If you've been instructed to use the Harvard referencing system and space your lines 1.5 points apart, that's what you have do to. But there is still room for originality, both in style (how you write) and form (the structure and format of your work). I will be discussing originality in presentations in Chapter 6.

Originality in form and style comes with a warning. Do not overdo it. There is a risk if you 'play around' too much that your work will be seen as bizarre. The reason I'm threatening you with this bucket of chilled water is that originality in style and form often – not always but often – lacks the perceived value and *caché* of originality of content. It is far easier to dismiss as superficial. To get a sense of what I'm warning about, and before I introduce you to some of the great things you *can* do with form and style, let's dive in at the deep end and make a poem.

Take a newspaper.

Take some scissors.

Choose from this paper an article the length you want to make your poem.

Cut out the article.

Next carefully cut out each of the words that make up this article and put them all in a bag.

Shake gently.

Next take out each cutting one after the other.

Copy conscientiously in the order in which they left the bag.

The poem will resemble you.

And there you are—an infinitely original author of charming sensibility, even though unappreciated by the vulgar herd.[4]

This is Tristan Tzara's 'To make a Dadaist Poem' from 1920. He was trying to spark a cultural revolution; he wasn't giving advice to students. What mark would you get if you did what Tzara suggests for your next assignment? It could be 100 per cent and it could be 0 per cent.

Let's look at some techniques that are less risky, that can and do work for students (for other examples see Chapter 1's discussion of

'Planning'). In each of them, the originality works because it communicates and amplifies the argument. As always with originality, your innovation should reflect and support your task, not distract from it.

Illustration

The most obvious thing you can do to enliven a text is incorporate illustrations, in the form of charts, maps, drawings, diagrams and photographs. In many disciplines, most student essays have no illustrations so any such addition may be seen as innovative. The likelihood of your images being considered original will increase if you devise and create them yourself. This is fine for photographs but for everything else, stop! Be careful. You can easily spend more time creating one graphic than writing 3000 words. Instead:

1. *Adapt your source material.* If it is a graph, rather than just reprinting it, simplify it and create your own version, which can be labelled 'adapted from [name of source]'.
2. *Make your images sweat.* Rather than just using them to illustrate a point, discuss and even critique them. Note how they are useful in some ways but limited in others, for example, how they are based on incomplete information, assumptions or bias. The tight-lipped and minimal 'see Figure 3.2' approach assumes the meaning of an illustration is obvious and, like a train ticket, merely provides visual proof of something. If you show that you have really thought about an image, your use of it is more likely to be seen as incisive and original. Write about what is going on in the image. This is especially useful with photographs, where you can pick out, for example, details in both background and foreground as well as composition in order to deepen your argument.
3. *Innovate types of images.* It is worth thinking about the range of visual forms, some of which might bring something extra to your work. Here's a short list of those not so far mentioned: cartoons, collages, advertisements, paintings, 3-D visualisations, film stills.

Voice and reflexivity

Reflexivity can be a site of originality, but not always. Writing about your own 'position', 'location' and identity in relation to your topic is more likely to be read as original if your treatment of this material is anchored in academic work and in specific themes. Sentences that start 'I think...' or 'As a White woman I experience...' sound clumsy and are not likely to be seen as innovative. Compare these constructions with: 'Drawing on the work of Blue, I interrogate my own racialised experience as an au pair as source material for a wider examination of the racialisation of care work'. This too is 'reflexive', it's autobiographical, but it's specific, critical, anchored, and it doesn't assume that the meaning of an identity is obvious or fixed in stone.

TRY THIS

Aim: To write about an image in an innovative way

Identify a photograph that is relevant to your area of study. Note down as many items from the following list as possible:

1. When, where and by whom was the image taken?
2. How do the composition, image details, design (use of medium, colour, etc.), foreground and background work to communicate an argument?
3. Are there ways in which the image is misleading or limited in its representation of its topic?
4. Using an image search function, are there similar or 'competing' images that tell us something different?

This exercise might result in just one or two lines of text, sometimes more, but in either case your use of the image will come to the fore. This will help embed good practice, ensuring you never again use an image as self-evident proof of something.

Examples of arts-based practice in the research process

Here I introduce a range of examples from different disciplines that show how different forms of arts-based practice have been used to collect information. They should be read as provocations, stimulating us to think not 'can I do the same?' but 'how can I adapt this?'. The forms of originality discussed in Chapters 2, 3 and 4 will help generate answers to that last question. Thus, for example, we might ask:

- Can I take this practice into a different geographical or historical context?
- Can I combine this practice with the insights of a specific theory or from another sub-field or discipline?
- Can I bring out something that is 'minor' in this example to make it centre stage?

Given so much academic work is done in teams over several years, it is also important to ask practical questions of these case studies. For example:

- How can I reframe this example for a lone research project that has to be undertaken within a few months?
- Is there *one* specific practice that I can pick out and work with from this example?

As these questions hint, the instances below are not models or destinations but points of departure.

Photos, maps and collage created by interviewees: Dawn Mannay's (2010) study of the lives of mothers and daughters on a UK 'council estate' sought to gain a 'nuanced understanding of the mothers' and daughters' worlds'.[5] To this end she asked her subjects to take photographs, make maps and create collages about local places that had meaning for them. These objects were then used as conversational cues in interviews. Thus, Mannay's interviews were not formatted in the traditional way as 'question and answer' (which can be limiting and lack depth), but were enabled and framed by her subjects' creativity and experiences:

> ...the use of participant-directed visual data production and the subsequent discussions tended to reveal far more than I would have expected using an entirely verbal approach for data production. The technique allowed time for the participants to reflect on their lives without the direction of an intrusive research voice.[6]

Children's drawings: Sara Eldén's (2013) Swedish study worked with young children and used 'draw-your-day' and 'concentric circles of closeness' drawing exercises to 'help the child and the researcher narrativize practices and relationships of care that would otherwise be obscured'.[7] For the 'circles', she asked the children to draw themselves 'in the inner circle, and then to draw people "who take care of you", "who you take care of" and "who are important to you" in the surrounding circles'. This type of exercise requires detailed explanatory narrative. Here is Eldén's description of one 'draw-your-day' exercise:

> When asked to draw his morning, Milo immediately, and with quite impressive detail, starts to describe the morning routine in the family. Soon he comes to think about the porridge he loves for breakfast, and decides to draw it. This inspires him to talk about who first taught him to make porridge – Anna – a friend of his mother's and whose son, Simon, often stays at Milo's house. These emerge as central relationships in Milo's life – both Anna as someone who provides practical care for him, and Simon whom Milo sees as part of his family, 'at least sometimes', and someone whom he, Milo, cares for (proudly). When drawing the porridge, he also makes a great deal out of telling me that he is quite capable of making his own porridge himself now.[8]

Patients' stories: Jennifer Lapum et al. (2011) studied patients' experiences of open-heart surgery by asking them to write stories at specific stages prior to and following their operation.[9] This US-based study had five phases and the stories were collected at each phase: pre-operative, post-operative, at discharge from hospital, early and later recovery at home. Key words, phrases and ideas from the patients' stories were categorised and used to create poems. The team then created a series of photographs that highlighted the main narrative ideas of each poem. This multiply creative analytic technique led towards a public exhibition, where the research findings were disseminated and the participants could see the results of their efforts.

Co-producing life stories with refugees and artists: Maggie O'Neill's (2008) UK-based ethnographic study used creative writing and visuals, facilitated by artists, to access the experiences of refugees. Thus, for example:

> [one] Afghan group wanted to explore their narratives in creative writing workshops and so we commissioned Exiled Writers Ink to facilitate this. A series of creative writing workshops were undertaken with Afghan refugees and asylum seekers led by Exiled Writers Ink. ... Both groups produced some incredible visual and poetic texts from their experiences of exile, displacement and the process of developing a sense of belonging in the new situation.[10]

Mandala drawings: Amy Blodgett et al. studied the sport experiences of young Canadian First Nation athletes who were moving off reserves to take part in sport. The research team included First Nation researchers, who developed and led the use of mandala drawings. It was they who

> suggested that this cultural link would improve the meaningfulness of the research for the athlete participants and help them share their stories more holistically. Though other culturally relevant art forms could have been used, such as beading, quilting, or drumming, the research team concluded that these methods were much less feasible than the mandala drawings, particularly in that they required art-specific skills and expertise that the team members did not have.[11]

Comic creation: In a course that explicitly encouraged creative output, student researcher Emily Thiessen used visual material gathered in her mother's home state in Indonesia to produce her assignment in comic form. Drawing on the tradition of comic story-tellers, like Joe Sacco, she inserted herself into the comic, implicitly and explicitly, in the edges of the panels. Thiessen explains: 'I aim to show that others' perspectives on resettlement are more central than mine by centering them in the frames.' However, she mixes reflexive and autobiographical elements into her practice, 'acknowledging' through various visual clues that her story 'has me doubly mixed into it; first altered by my presence, and later told from my point of view'.[12]

TRY THIS

Aim: Trying out arts-based practice

This is about making notes, jotting down ideas, rather than actually starting arts-based practice. You want to know what might work and how it might help you. Select one of the examples introduced above and note down how it could be reshaped for your own research interests or assignment topic. For under-graduate students, this will have to involve picking out just one or two elements and severely limiting the timescale of the research. Next, using one of the tech-niques identified in Chapters 2, 3 or 4, identify what innovation you are bringing to this particular element, i.e., how you are adding to it and/or critiquing it.

Arts-based practice: Critical questions

There are good reasons for students to take seriously the idea of incor-porating creative practice into their work. It can make your work stand out and is often seen as original. However, asking critical questions of arts-based practice will help you arrive at more incisive ways of 'working with' arts-based approaches or, indeed, for deciding not to adopt this approach. Despite the recent explosion of arts-based practice in some areas, it is important to understand that there are many ways of being original and the function and utility of the arts pathway is not self-evident and requires interrogation.

The most pressing of these critical questions for students are practical ones. But they also bring forward wider inconsistencies between an arts-based approach and the intellectual and social ambitions of scholarship.

Practical challenges: Creative practice can take a lot of time and can distract from one's central task. Incorporating it into any piece of work requires careful time-management and consideration of how it is helping you communicate your argument and evidence. Creative practice that is tangential, eccentric or irrelevant is likely to lose you marks.

Wider questions: Within some disciplines, notably in some fields within psy-chology, education and anthropology, arts-based practice has proven value. However, the political claims made for it can be challenged. Engaging confidently in arts-based work – leading it and knowing how it fits within the wider terrain of culture, including modern art – requires high levels of language proficiency and cultural capital. Thus, arts-based narratives have an awkward relationship with transnational and transcultural communication. More specifically, and reflecting the fact that arts-based practice is, overwhelmingly, a Western phenomenon, international, non-Western voices have tended to be absent from arts-based research agendas. We can also question how effective arts-based practice is in empowering marginalised and minority groups. If one's aim is to influence policy and/or enable long-term change, arts-based work, with its ephemeral events that involve tiny groups of people, may not appear an effective option.

The wider epistemological and pedagogical implications of an arts-based research paradigm can also be questioned. The attraction to art among non-art-based scholars appears to be bound up with its capacity to register and express 'many truths'. Explaining why researchers should adopt these methods, Helen Kara (2015) explains that '"truth" may be as complex as artists suggest – multiple, partial, context-dependent, and contingent'.[13] Thus arts-based work is associated with giving value to, and not judging, multiple viewpoints and experiences. But what are the consequences of chipping away at, or entirely giving up on, the idea that some truths are more accurate than others or that expertise is of more value than opinion? If arts-based practice is aligned to relativism, then it subverts attempts to communicate the objective reality of issues, such as inequality and climate change. It is also worth asking how student 'art work' can be assessed in a fair manner, especially in an intellectual environment dominated by relativism. The less consistent and less clearly formulated assessment criteria are, the more open the marking process is to social bias and personal favouritism.

Originality in the creative disciplines

Creative disciplines (which include art, performance, graphics, fashion and creative writing) combine creative practice with essay writing, exams and presentations. The techniques offered in the previous chapters can be applied to these 'non-creative' assessments. It is only in respect to creative practice itself that distinct advice is required, and even here, there is less difference than might be imagined. Originality remains, in all cases, a process of 'working with', of adding to and engaging. In fact, the most striking difference between the creative disciplines and non-creative disciplines is a perverse one, namely that across the former there is a tendency to shy away from claims to originality, even to the point of refusing its existence. For some artists and writers it is almost a point of pride to claim there is 'nothing new'. For Mark Twain, 'There is no such thing as a new idea. It is impossible.

We simply take a lot of old ideas and put them into a sort of mental kaleidoscope'.[14] The film maker Jim Jarmusch provides a similarly arresting image:

> Nothing is original. Steal from anywhere that resonates with inspiration or fuels your imagination. Devour old films, new films, music, books, paintings, photographs, poems, dreams, random conversations, architecture, bridges, street signs, trees, clouds, bodies of water, light and shadows. Select only things to steal from that speak directly to your soul. If you do this, your work (and theft) will be authentic. Authenticity is invaluable; originality is nonexistent.[15]

Less dramatic and more accurate terms for what Jarmusch calls 'stealing' and 'devouring' are 'working with' and 'adding to'. Twain and Jarmusch's dismissal of originality derives from an understanding of it as something that comes from nothing. This is not a convincing definition. Originality exists: without it there would be no change and no progress. These dismissals channel anxiety rather than insight. It is a nervousness found across the creative arts. In the humanities and social sciences 'originality' is a specified criterion for the best marks. In striking contrast, looking through many assessment criteria in, for example, fine art, I find that the word 'originality' is noticeable for its absence. Here are the criteria for the highest marks from one fine arts degree course:

> Successfully integrates the elements, processes and procedures relating to the challenges of the brief
>
> Engages with practice as a creative process within a broader community of practitioners
>
> Sees engaging in practice as an act of developing a personal world-view. (mark awarded: 70–100)

Here we see an emphasis on integration and engagement and, by implication, consistency and commitment. It would appear that, when awarding the top marks in fine art at this institution, originality does not matter. But, of course, it does. It matters a lot, but it is going by other names. In this case, its most direct reference takes the form of 'developing a personal world-view'. In other rubrics, we find 'risk-taking', and/or the development of a 'personal style' or 'distinctive style', being named and valorised. But originality is invisibly present in many ways. How, after all, is 'success' in the skills of integration, engagement, consistency and commitment to be measured? It is, in large part, by what distinct form and personal style you are bringing to – adding to – these processes. If you are just repeating a formula, copying across, your work will not stand out and will not get into the 70–100 band.

If originality is important, why is it not being named? There are three reasons. The first is that assessing creativity is a highly subjective process. This leads to assessment becoming a site of unease. An emphasis on clearly observable characteristics, such as engagement and integration, mitigates this problem. To put it another way, overt reference to originality is banished because it draws attention to the unwelcome fact that the marking process is questionable. The second reason is that in the arts, talk of originality is hackneyed. It reflects a popular stereotype of the arts and art students as unconventional, or at least not easily corralled by conservative institutions like universities. The third reason is that explicitly encouraging originality in the arts opens a Pandora's box of unwanted consequences. It is associated with encouraging solipsism and self-regard, and thus a lack of knowledge, skill and consistency.

The creative disciplines are diverse and there are occasions and courses where originality is not a useful ambition. In skill and technique-based work, such as acting, for example, it is probably better to keep originality for your essays. In other areas, however, originality can complement your ambitions to be creative, to develop your own style and to show a willingness to take risks. The following four examples of creative practice all exhibit originality, and it is this that explains their impact and influence. However, in each case, this originality is a consequence of their engagement and connectedness within existing traditions. Students' work usually exists in portfolio form, or with accompanying narrative context, which allow these kinds of engagement and connection to be spelled out.

Art as social practice. Example: Assemble.[16] This UK-based art group work across the fields of art, design and architecture to create projects in tandem with the communities who use them. Their architectural spaces and environments promote direct action and embrace a DIY sensibility. Their most famous intervention was the Granby Four Streets project in Liverpool, a collaboration with the residents of a rundown council housing estate to clean up their neighbourhood, paint empty houses and establish a local market. Granby Four Streets involved the renovation of 10 houses and a series of empty shops, planting and creating social outdoor spaces, and offering building jobs and training to local people. Assemble also facilitated a workshop selling homeware made in collaboration with local artists and craftspeople.

The idea of artists as socially engaged was an important facet of twentieth-century art. In the later decades of the century, collaborative and community-based art came to the fore. Assemble take these existing traditions to a new level, effectively re-imagining the artist as a literal builder of communities. Moreover, this is not a short-term engagement: 'You have to spend years developing relationships', says

Rick Lowe. 'It'd be an arrogant disregard of a community to come in and think you can grasp all the complexities of a place in a short time.'[17]

Re-imagining tradition: Example: Yu Qiping. Many of the Chinese artist Yu Qiping's paintings look, at first glance, like traditional handscroll paintings of court scenes, complete with pre-modern costume, landscape, linework and muted palette.[18] Yu Qiping's work is consistent but also consistently ambiguous. The images demand a double-take. They slip readily into the surreal. In 'Let's talk about ordinary' (2021), a monk figure stares happily at a wall through which a menacing black tree is bursting. Other paintings are disconcertingly sensual, such as 'Intoxicated in aromatherapy', in which an 'intoxicated' monk or scholar figure writhes beneath a thin plume of smoke.[19]

Yu Qiping is working with a traditional Chinese art form; indeed, working with it so closely that he appears to be playing a game with its style and possibility. The promise of mutation and transgression is always present, waiting to push through the walls. However, the work refuses easy categorisation, such as placement within surrealism or other Western avant-garde traditions. It is both removed from tradition, dislocated and distant from the past, yet also immersive, inviting us back into its lost world.

Working with Existentialism and Absurdism: Example: 'Blasted', a play by Sarah Kane.[20] The play is set in a hotel room – 'the kind that is so expensive it could be anywhere in the world' – where its small cast of foul-mouthed and unpleasant characters (the opening line is: 'I've shat in better places that this') throw pithy, brutalised and often racist statements at each other during and after nihilistic acts of drinking and sex, before a brutal closing scene where the hotel is bombed.

'Blasted' strikes notes that chime with many important works in modern theatre. Its pared down, pithy, language has strong echoes of Samuel Becket; so too its jarring juxtaposition of events, which reference a wider tradition of absurdist theatre. There are also resonances with traditions of British political theatre, notably those in which the focus is brutality and brutalisation (such as Edward Bond's 'Saved'). These influences are not hard to see, yet the way Kane works with these traditions is distinctive: she brings a visceral feminist politics to their staging, turning Existentialism and Absurdism into a mirror of physical and social violence.

Environmentalist fashion: The clothes designer Juliana Garcia Bello uses disused and discarded material, combined with raw cotton, to make her garments.[21] Her method has four elements: upcycling (the practice of extending the life of objects); handmade (to 'ensure every piece is durable, low-impact, comfortable and timeless, the garments are made in a simple way with handmade details'); reconstruction (Bello's fabrics are obtained through donations and deadstock from organisations, stores and companies); and community (Bello helps people learn how to extend the useful life of garments by sharing videos and workshops).

Bello's work reflects the wider turn towards social engagement seen in many creative disciplines. In her case, she brings in principles from environmentalism and, more specifically, critiques of the short lifespan of modern clothes, to create a coherent, engaged and innovative brand.

Conclusions

Throughout this book we have seen that originality emerges from engagement. This is also true for those working with the arts. Some disciplines are less open than others to arts-based practice and some students will not encounter a single course in their degree that encourages or even acknowledges its use. In many others, though, it is explicitly endorsed and there is an increasing number of courses where arts-based work is required and assessed. These different scenarios present different challenges for students. In the latter case, where arts-based work is required, the challenge is how to present work that will succeed, meet the brief and be judged original. My answer to the question 'how?' will, by now, not be surprising: students need to anchor their work in existing arts-based innovations and clearly signal how they are adding to – and this can include critiquing – these examples. Original work does not just repeat, but it takes and moves forward. This is not just turning the 'kaleidoscope'. It is even more misguided to call it 'stealing', since this implies that we should take without acknowledgment. This is poor practice and, given that most creative workers are happy to discuss their influences, it is doubly implausible. Don't 'steal', engage.

For students who are attracted to arts-based work but find that there is little explicit encouragement for it in their taught courses, the best option is to establish whether there is room to develop it within self-led courses, such as the dissertation. If there is, then the mere fact of applying arts-based practice is likely to be seen as original. Thus, the rarity of arts-based practice can be made to work in your favour. However, even if it is not common, it remains the case that any such intervention should be anchored in the existing literature. Originality must always refer backwards in order to point forwards.

6

Presentations, Group Work, Dissemination and Impact: Opportunities for Originality

Introduction

Students are assessed in an increasingly diverse range of ways. In this chapter I look first at how originality can arise from and improve group work, oral presentations, posters and podcasts. I will then address one of the potentially most innovative aspects of the contemporary student experience, namely dissemination and impact. If academics want to get a research grant, or get promoted, they *have* to show that they aren't confined by the 'ivory tower'; that they are engaged with wider publics. Today this orientation, fitfully, unevenly, but surely, is shaping the design of teaching curricula and providing opportunities, at both undergraduate and postgraduate level, for students to think more broadly about who all their hard work is for.

Presentations

In presentations, your focus – the thing that absorbs most of your work – should be on scholarly originality. You need to explain to your audience how you are adding to, working with, and anchoring your ideas. It is useful to spell out your innovation at the start and, in presentations, it is especially important to do so at the end. Make your conclusion bold and clear: it is the most important place to concisely deliver your 'take-away'.

Originality in presentations is better thought of in terms of intellectual content rather than in terms of the many formats and technologies that could liven up your visuals. GIFs, cartoons, short films, audience participation, using a diversity of images, such as maps and infographics, and so on, can all make your talk more engaging. They may well get you extra marks for presentational skills. This is good news but our focus is on originality. It is better to think of these diverse formats and technologies as communicative skills rather than as adding to the academic originality of your presentation. This may sound like I'm splitting hairs but it's a distinction that is worth paying attention to, for two reasons. First, it encourages you to use eye-catching inserts judiciously and not to make the mistake of thinking that the gimmickier your presentation is the more original it will appear. Second, effective academic presentations need substantive academic content; this is the foundation of success, especially success in delivering an innovative intervention in an academic debate. Your presentational skills should be at the service of this intervention, not take precedence over them.

So if you want to give an original presentation, don't bring a guitar, don't have visuals that pulse like a 1970s disco, and don't structure your 10 minutes as a pub quiz. All those things could work in other contexts and are maybe just the job if that kind of creativity is explicitly encouraged by your course leaders (if they tell you to bring maracas, then bring maracas). But, in most cases, they do not contribute enough to justify the risk they incur of going wrong and of bewildering your audience. So keep the visuals clear, the pace even, and the argument and structure upfront and succinct. The communicative basics should be solid, providing a platform for the originality of your ideas and research.

Posters

All the points made above in respect to presentations apply to posters. Keep the originality to the content. Using obscure fonts in odd colours will not be seen as original but as frustrating. The title of a poster is its key 'hook' and your claim to innovation should, if possible, be contained in it. This may involve using words such as 'new', 'post', or some other clear 'key words' (see Chapter 3) that signal that your ideas are ambitious and your poster is offering more than mere description. The visual logic of posters needs to be simple and clear. It is a good idea to have a bold conclusion statement, which is often placed bottom right. This should not just repeat your title but spell out what you have shown or argued and how this has challenged, added to and otherwise 'worked with' existing ideas and traditions.

Podcasts and other recordings

Audio and audio-visual formats open a vast terrain for innovation. In audio work, different forms of narrative, voice, ambient sounds, shifts and overlays can all be used. There are several useful online 'how to' resources for students making podcasts.[1] Although audio-visual work has an even greater array of potential elements, in practice it largely takes the form of recordings of slide-show presentations, using the same software that staff use to teach remotely. Such presentations should follow the general guidance under 'Presentations'.

In both podcasts and filmed work, you need to attend to the assignment outline and criteria very carefully. Having done so, it is time to think about innovations. As so often with originality, less is more. It is better to use one or two techniques effectively and with nuance than layer numerous ones into your work. Innovation should always flow from the needs of your tasks and topic, otherwise it will appear superficial and distracting. Where your assignment is based on teamwork, then the four-stage plan introduced below can be adapted for use. It is likely that this adaption will need to take into consideration the different skills of your group, as some students will have prior experience of broadcasting and filming and some will have none. It should not be assumed that the former group take the lead, for the results will be judged largely in terms of the power of your ideas, engagement and communicative capacities rather than as technical exercises.

Group work

Group work is not always welcomed by students who want to innovate. This prejudice rests on a stereotype of originality as a unique, individual contribution. Group work is sometimes cast as the opposite, as a committee thing, as a hammering out of a shared position in which the distinctive, bold or novel is bashed down and a lowest common dominator – the thing you all mange to agree on – is grudgingly accepted.

This stereotype is way off the mark. In their overview of 'teaching originality', Scheffer et al. advise students to 'team up with people who have different mindsets'. They argue that 'group diversity' can be intrinsically beneficial.[2] The group can be thought of as a foundry of ideas, in which people spark off each other and something new can be born, something unobtainable by lone endeavour. When it comes to originality, group work should be approached as an opportunity and a resource. After all, as we have seen, originality is not a mystic or solitary act; it takes labour and it reflects engagement. More specifically, surveying the literature on a topic, in order to identify and develop an innovative contribution, requires hours of labour and a preparedness to be open to the ideas of others. The group can not only generate new ideas but also radically expand the hours you have to explore them.

In a typical scenario, where the group is tasked with producing a conventional academic output, such as an essay, or presentation, there are four stages to effective and innovative group work. The first sounds easy: for everyone to agree that the group is working towards an innovative engagement with an existing theory, argument or body of evidence. This may sound too obvious to be worth stating but don't skip this stage. It makes sure you are all on the same page and it steers and coheres the aim of your group, away from mere description or regurgitation and towards something more ambitious. Stage two: the group needs to generate ideas on the topic you have chosen or been allocated (see Chapter 1: 'Reading and generating ideas'). You may agree quite quickly about what idea you are going to work with. Alternatively – and this is not a worse option, just different – you will want to arrive at a short list (as short as possible) of possible options. Stage three: this is when you individually go off and explore your chosen idea or ideas. If you have all agreed on the same one, then each team member should research different aspects or approaches to it (so you don't replicate work). If you have not agreed, and have several possibilities, then each team member should be assigned one which they will then scope out. Stage four: you come back and decide on the idea, or the specific approach to your agreed idea, which is the most promising. What does 'promising' look like? It means that this is the idea that excites you and that you think you can add value to. You can use the techniques introduced in Chapters 2 to 5 to help guide this process. Any and all of these stages may need to be repeated. Of course, you still have to decide on the form of your assignment and how you will divide your labour to complete it. That all matters, and has to be got right, but it's organisational rather than intellectual work. If you adopt the four-stage approach described, or something like it, you can be confidant that, academically, your work stands a good chance of being considered original.

Anyone with experience of teamwork might be rolling their eyes. It can be frustrating and it's not your fault if you find yourself partnered up with people who are zombie-scrolling their phone or find some other way to absent themselves. If you find yourself stuck in such a situation, then the four-point plan sketched above can still help, as it provides a structure that, hopefully, can force the hand of slackers. Having a clear division of labour and a clear ambition to do more than just describe and illustrate, but to engage and innovate, may not fully solve but should ameliorate the problem of free riders.

Dissemination and impact

Academics are worried they aren't being listened to. 'Dissemination' and 'impact' are major concerns in most universities today (they also help explain the turn to 'creative' and 'arts-based' forms of research discussed in Chapter 5). In my experience, students are no less concerned about dissemination and impact. The idea that all that labour, all those months of research, just gets stamped with a mark and filed away is troubling.

Thinking about dissemination and impact is not just worthwhile but is also an innovative thing for students to do and it can look great on your CV/resumé. Although many higher education institutions have 'impact strategies' and 'public engagement' initiatives, students may not feel they have the time, the resources or the official encouragement to get involved in this kind of work. But a new mood is abroad and it is worthwhile, before we look at some examples of the things you can do to disseminate your work and have impact, to introduce this evolving context. It is a significant shift, one that promises to change how students experience higher education. Today many colleges claim 'community engagement' as an aspect, and sometimes a major part, of their 'offer'. For example, Lincoln University promises to develop 'meaningful student engagement, both within and beyond the curriculum, including opportunities for proactive co-creation, partnership, and collaboration'.[3] The University of Texas, in collaboration with the City of San Antonio, organises 'science fiestas' as a 'platform for scientists to inform, engage, and excite the public, while providing graduate students a unique opportunity for practical training in communication, leadership and project management'.[4] Outreach and engagement has also made its way into specific degree courses, sometimes as a stand-alone module. For example, in my own department in Newcastle University, one of the most innovative and admired courses is 'Community Volunteering: A Geography Perspective'.[5] The module outline explains that it involves:

> doing Geography in partnership with local organizations (70 hours, group placement) [and] learning and practising skills of community organizing and coalition building (on a continuum of volunteering, advocacy, and activism).

What all these examples tell us is that the importance of dissemination and impact is increasingly understood and accepted. More specifically, even modest forays in this diverse field are likely to be well received and considered pioneering.

What forms do dissemination and impact take? There is a continuum. At one end are activities designed to get your name and your work 'out there'; at the other end are activities in which you work with others, such as a community group, and aim to give them voice and profile. However, this selfish-to-selfless spectrum doesn't quite capture the reality, for all these techniques involve engagement and students can gain profile and benefit from even the most community-minded of them. Here is a short list of different types of dissemination and impact:

Feedback: disseminating your research findings (often in short, summary form) back to the people you used to facilitate access to your field and/or interviewed is good practice. If they are initial findings, their reactions can then be incorporated into your finished research.

Community engagement and presentation: opportunities for such work can flow from your research or from your own outreach. They can take the form of a one-off talk to a local community group, flyers or social media messages distributed locally. More ambitious interventions include long-term volunteering or kick-starting a festival, co-organised with local people and other students.

Blogs, social media and website: having a targeted approach, in which you focus your updates and tweets on a specific field of interest, will give your work more impact than personal or general messages. Similarly, a topic-focused website will have far more hits than one that centres on you. Include links to other sites and to key papers on the topic.

Press article: you can pitch a piece to an international news website or your local student magazine and, in both cases, you need a thick skin. Most pitches get rebuffed (which in the world of journalism, usually means you get no reply). In order to get a piece accepted, it has to be focused, 'of the moment' and intriguing. Being 'of the moment' can be as simple as pitching around an anniversary. For example, 'this year is the fiftieth anniversary of "Science City"' creates a hook to peg an article on. Finding a punchy title is key. Try to find the name of the editor you are pitching to. The more direct, 'of the moment' and specific the pitch the better your chances.

Academic article: many academic journals have sections for short (often about 1000–1500 words) pieces, called 'interventions', 'commentaries' or something similar. Contact the editor of this section (they often have separate editors but not always) by email and pitch an idea to them. The more specific the idea, the more it appears to engage and add to an existing debate in a specific sub-field, the bet-ter the chance of a positive reply. Once submitted, your piece is quite likely to be rejected. This usually happens because it is outside the journal's remit, or because it is poorly written, badly referenced, incoherent or lacks substance. But sometimes authors are just unlucky. Don't take it personally: every author can show you wads of rejection letters.

TIP

Concrete claims, not wishful ones

Claims about dissemination and impact have to be realistic and commensurate with the scale and ambition of your work. And they should to be concrete: they need to refer to things you have either done or are in the process of doing. Claiming you *will* do something – one day – is rarely convincing.

Your ability to do any of these things depends on the time you have available. Postgraduate students are best placed to engage in dissemination and impact. PhD students *should* be undertaking at least one of the approaches noted above, and MA students can certainly benefit from them. Undergraduate students often find that it is only during dissertation research that they can afford the time to engage in any of these approaches. Traditionally, undergraduates were not expected to be thinking about dissemination and impact. But, as we have seen, this is changing. It is a reorientation designed to benefit both students and the wider society, helping students see pathways for their work beyond their degree and helping establish universities as a civic resource.

Another word of caution: engaging in impact and dissemination tends to be exciting and absorbing; students need to be careful not to get distracted from their assignment tasks. It is a good idea to contact course leaders to tell them of your intentions and get advice. Once done, don't keep your successes to yourself: let teaching staff, tutors, friends and family know about your website, a piece in the local newspaper or similar. When it comes to impact and dissemination, there is no point in being shy.

CASE STUDY I

Assignment: Undergraduate dissertation

Form of dissemination: Feedback and press coverage

Sample sentences:

An outline synopsis of my findings was distributed to interviewees.

(Continued)

These policy recommendations were presented to the business I studied by means of a short PowerPoint presentation.

Interest in the topic was also generated by a short feature I wrote for *The Local Newspaper*.

These examples are concrete: they point to things done or soon to be done and they are not wildly ambitious. Writing 'I *will* disseminate this research' or 'I *will* contact community groups' may be sincere but sounds far less impressive.

CASE STUDY II

Discipline: History

Form of dissemination: Research website

Here is an extract from a PhD student website that both records their research and is designed to attract participants:

This project is interested in how the experience of growing up in the North East has changed over the last 40 or so years. It aims to preserve and deepen our understandings of North East heritage by capturing stories of childhood from local communities. … We want to gather intergenerational stories to chart and understand how changes in the North East since the 1980s have affected childhoods.[6]

The website is titled 'North East Childhoods' and, at every turn, is specific about its focus. It also includes links to 'partner projects' and 'participant information'.

CASE STUDY III

Discipline: Medicine

Form of dissemination: A student community outreach project

The Covid pandemic isolated students but it also energised many to initiate a range of community outreach services. An overview of these medical student-led initiatives in the USA makes for inspiring reading:

one student-led initiative involved weekly check-ups, phone calls, or video calls with older adults at local, underserved nursing homes to not only provide social support during their isolation but also enhance their physical and mental health through medical counselling. Other groups ... created and translated public health pamphlets in multiple languages for diverse community members across the country. Other students who were passionate about technology and hands-on projects initiated the 3D printing of face masks to address the nationwide shortage of PPE and masks. ... Although these student-led initiatives and extracurriculars may not directly stem from a medical school's standard curriculum, these student initiatives leverage web-based resources and are vital to medical students' education as they serve their communities and deliver compassion.[7]

I include this overview as a case study, even though it depicts a wide array of activities by many students, because it signals both the ambition and capacity of students to have impact. And although medical students have a particular skillset, so too, for example, do history students or business students.

TRY THIS

Aim: Create a research website

Use a free website builder to construct a one-page profile on a topic that you will be working on. Resist the temptation to fill the site with lots of other ideas and interests. If it looks like a website that is not about a specific topic but just about you, and/or a whole bunch of things, it will not attract clicks and will not serve its purpose. The site's key words need to be clear, repeated, distinct and innovative. There is no point having a site titled 'sociology'. A site called 'youth, race and identity in Scotland' stands a better chance of having impact. Make sure you include references to key academic work and links to other sites as well as your social media and contact details. Links make links: if you link to others they may link to you (especially if you politely ask them to). It will take weeks, or months, for search engines to start finding your site. If you're writing an essay on the topic your website covers, you can cite your website (but don't overdo 'self-citation'; once is enough).

TRY THIS

Aim: Give a public presentation

During your dissertation or thesis research process approach a community group and volunteer to give a talk about your work. If this event can happen before the completion of your research, you can refer to it in your text. Since so many people think that giving a public talk is too scary to even contemplate, it is important to be honest with your target group and yourself. You're a student, you have some material that may interest the group, you are giving a short, informal talk, and perhaps you can open up a conversation afterwards on the topic. It is a bit scary – of course it is – but is it beyond you? You're not being assessed, your talk can be just 15 minutes and, in all likelihood, you'll have a small but friendly audience.

Conclusion

This chapter has covered a diverse range of opportunities for originality. In each case, I have tried to steer you away from the outlandish and general and towards the engaged and the specific. Whether you are shaping a presentation or pitching a piece to a newspaper, you need to choose your words carefully. It will help to look back at Chapter 3, especially its advice about how you can communicate your central innovation. It is this that your audience will alight on. In a way, this chapter has been about the simplest types of originality, because in each case (with the exception of group work) you don't have the space or time for elaboration. Your take-away point, your innovation, needs to be there at the start and at the end. It does not need to be earth-shattering: it is better to have a believable, robust yet modest point than to over claim. It is not convincing to tell people they 'will never see the world in the same way again', but you can credibly claim to have reframed and reimagined one specific aspect of it.

Staying Original

Originality is a thing we constantly clamour for, and constantly quarrel with.

Thomas Carlyle[1]

In Chapter 1 I wrote that originality is 'not a product of age but of engagement'. This cuts both ways: the youngest student can be original and so can the oldest. There are many clichés about originality and one of the most persistent associates it with youth and, by association, casts everyone over 35 as incapable of innovation. Perhaps it is because of the rising number of old people across the world, but this stereotype is no longer convincing. Originality is something within reach not just right now but at any time in our lives.

This book is designed for students so they produce better work and get better marks. It has offered tips and techniques that will make your efforts stand out. But, just below the surface, there is more going on. By showing that originality is just another skill, How to Be Original burns away the mysterious aura and the glamour that has been woven round it. I've 'disenchanted' originality and, I would argue, this can help empower people as they negotiate and try to make sense of a society which appears to prize originality above all else yet continues to treat it as unexplainable and unobtainable. Today, having a 'unique selling point' is demanded of everything and everybody. It is an exhausting and impossible demand, not only because it is so pervasive, but because originality continues to be treated as a kind of magic, something that happens by chance or erupts from flashes of genius.

If originality is not beyond you – and it isn't – then the world becomes a less intimidating place. This reinforces the idea that How to Be Original is a book that today's students may find useful at many stages of their life. Whether it is a job interview, developing a product line, or being a social activist, the question of what you can 'bring' to the situation is always going to be asked. We have seen how to answer that question, again and again, across pages of case studies and sample sentences: you engage, add to and 'work with' existing traditions and innovations.

But my attempt to 'disenchant' originality also presents a more general challenge. Modern societies define themselves as engines of originality: they keep chucking out more and more ideas and things. We all swim in the resultant ocean of stuff, much of it disposed of and discarded. A culture that privileges originality does not just produce nice shiny useful things, it also creates mountains of unwanted, unfashionable and decaying ones. Capitalism is the predominant economic mechanism of this churning Behemoth, but all forms of 'radicalism', all those exciting revolutions and insurrectionary ideas, are also part of it, whirring away in the production of 'the new'. This ensemble of diverse energies manu-factures constant change and constant uncertainty.

As long as we are in awe of originality, transfixed by novelty and associate all things new with all things better, this monster will keep growing. The current environmental crisis demands that we see it for what it is and begin to disabuse its myths. When a new skyline is bolted in place, and a recently built one is pulled down, and when yet another update appears in a product line, our eyes should not widen with wonder. There is no mystery at work. We have learnt something else too: that innova-tion can take many pathways. In fact, it might be more original to preserve those buildings or to ensure products can be mended and not thrown away. Originality is a tool and a technique, not a spell or sign of genius, and we can make use of it for better ends or for worse.

Notes

Chapter 1

1. André Gorz, 1972, 'Proceedings from a public debate organized in Paris by *Club de Nouvelle Observateur*', *Nouvelle Observateur*, 397, 19 June. Giorgos Kallis, 2018, *Degrowth*, Colombia University Press, New York.
2. Marten Scheffer, Matthijs Baas and Tone K. Bjordam, 2017, 'Teaching originality? Common habits behind creative production in science and arts', *Ecology and Society*, 22(2), 29. I have adapted Scheffer et al.'s work despite rather than because they take a romantic and 'exceptionalist' view of originality and use people like Darwin and Newton as their templates. Students do not have to instigate a scientific revolution to be original, nor do they have to emulate the habits of well-known geniuses. Scheffer et al.'s approach reflects a long tradition of identifying originality with genius. See, for example, T. Sharper Knowlson, 1920, *Originality: A Popular Study of the Creative Mind*, T. Werner Laurie, London.
3. Karolina Doughty, 2013, 'Walking together: The embodied and mobile production of a therapeutic landscape', *Health and Place*, 24, 140–146.
4. See Alastair Bonnett, 2004, *The Idea of the West: Culture, Politics and History*, Palgrave Macmillan, Basingstoke.
5. I am not using 'conservative' as a political term. Here it means practices that preserve and reproduce existing norms.
6. Cited by Andrew Reitz, 2021, Michael Ignatieff: thinking for yourself in a university is not easy', *Times Higher Education*, 27 October, https://www.timeshighereducation.com/news/michael-ignatieff-thinking-yourself-university-not-easy
7. Cited by anonymous, 1786, 'Anecdotes of Voltaire', *The Edinburgh Magazine: Volume 3*, J. Sibbald, Edinburgh, pp. 409–412, p. 410.

Chapter 2

1. Kimberlé W. Crenshaw, 2017, *On Intersectionality: Essential Writings*, The New Press, New York. Immanuel Maurice Wallerstein, 2004,

World-systems Analysis: An Introduction, Duke University Press, Durham, NC.

2. Elleke Boehmer, 2009, 'Edward Said and (the postcolonial occlusion of) gender', in B. Ghosh, *Edward Said and the Literary, Social and Political World*, Routledge, London.

3. Andre Gunder Frank, 1966, *The Development of Underdevelopment*, Monthly Review Press, New York; 1967, *Capitalism and Underdevelopment in Latin America*, Monthly Review Press, New York.

4. Rebecca E. Lee, Kristen McAlexander and Jorge Banda, 2011, *Reversing the Obesogenic Environment*, Human Kinetics, Champaign, IL.

Chapter 3

1. Nigel Thrift, 1996, *Spatial Formations*, Sage, London. Benjamin Noys, 2010, *Persistence of the Negative: A Critique of Contemporary Continental Theory*, Edinburgh University Press, Edinburgh. Timothy Lenton et al., 2008, 'Tipping elements in the Earth's climate system', *Proceedings of the National Academy of Sciences*, 105(6), 1786–1793.

2. Richard Florida, 2002, *The Rise of the Creative Class: And How it's Transforming Work, Leisure, Community and Everyday Life*, Perseus Book Group, New York.

3. Immanuel Wallerstein, 2004, *World-systems Analysis: An Introduction*, Duke University Press, Durham, NC. Alf Hornborg, 1998, 'Ecosystems and World Systems: Accumulation as an ecological process', *Journal of World-Systems Research*, 4(2), 169–177.

4. Stephen May (Ed.), 1999, *Critical Multiculturalism: Rethinking Multicultural and Antiracist Education*, Falmer Press, London. Debito Arudou, 2015, *Embedded Racism: Japan's Visible Minorities and Racial Discrimination*, Lexington Books, Lanham, MD. Arun Saldanha, 2007, *Psychedelic White: Goa Trance and the Viscosity of Race*, University of Minnesota Press, Minneapolis, MN.

5. Erwin Schrödinger, 1944, *What is Life? The Physical Aspect of the Living Cell*, Cambridge University Press, Cambridge, p. 22.

6. Pierre Bourdieu, 1977, 'Cultural reproduction and social reproduction', in J. Karabel and A. H. Halsey (Eds.), *Power and Ideology in Education*, Oxford University Press, New York, pp. 487–511; 1986, 'The forms of capital', in J. Richardson (Ed.), *Handbook of Theory and Research for the Sociology of Education*, Greenwood Press, New York, pp. 241–258.

7. Noam Chomsky, 1997, 'Noise: Noam Chomsky interviewed by Fred Branfman', https://chomsky.info/199702__/, accessed 6/11/2022.

8. Ferdinand Tönnies, 1887, *Gemeinschaft und Gesellschaft*, Fues's Verlag, Leipzig. Translated into English as *Fundamental Concepts of Sociology (Gemeinschaft und Gesellschaft)*, American Book Co., New York.

9. More precisely, Agamben is redefining the term 'sovereign power', while 'bare life' appears to be his own creation.
10. Giorgio Agamben, 1998, *Homo Sacer: Sovereign Power and Bare Life*, Stanford University Press, Stanford, CA. Giorgio Agamben, 1995, *Homo sacer. Il potere sovrano e la nuda vita*, Einaudi, Torino.
11. André Bourguignon, 1992, *Translating Freud*, Yale University Press, New Haven, CT.
12. Frank Dikötter, 1992, *The Discourse of Race in Modern China*, Stanford University Press, Stanford, CA.
13. Pamela Crossley, 1990, 'Thinking about ethnicity in early modern China', *Late Imperial China*, 11(1), 1–34.

Chapter 4

1. A. Alexandra Michel, 2007, 'A distributed cognition perspective on newcomers' change processes: The management of cognitive uncertainty in two investment banks', *Administrative Science Quarterly*, 52(4), 507–557, pp. 514–515.
2. Michael Stubbs, 2005, 'Conrad in the computer: Examples of quantitative stylistic methods, *Language and Literature*, 14(1), 5–24, p. 5, p. 22.
3. Jennifer Rowsell, 2011, 'Carrying my family with me: Artifacts as emic perspectives', *Qualitative Research*, 11(3), 331–346, p. 334, p. 344.
4. Caterina Arcidiacono, Daria Grimaldi, Salvatore Di Martino and Fortuna Procentese, 2016, 'Participatory visual methods in the "Psychology loves Porta Capuana' project", *Action Research*, 14(4), 376–392.
5. Chad Hammond, Wendy Gifford, Roanne Thomas, Seham Rabaa, Ovini Thomas and Marie-Cécile Domecq, 2018, 'Arts-based research methods with indigenous peoples: An international scoping review', *AlterNative: An International Journal of Indigenous Peoples*, 14(3), 260–276, p. 260.
6. Roser Beneito-Montagut, 2011, 'Ethnography goes online: Towards a user-centred methodology to research interpersonal communication on the internet', *Qualitative Research* 11(6), 716–735.
7. Geoff Payne, 2014, 'Surveys, statisticians and sociology: A history of (a lack of) quantitative methods', *Enhancing Learning in the Social Sciences*, 6(2), 74–89, p. 75.
8. Gillian Symon, Catherine Cassell and Rosie Dickson, 2000, 'Expanding our research and practice through innovative research methods', *European Journal of Work and Organizational Psychology*, 9(4), 457–462. Gillian Symon and Catherine Cassell, 1999, 'Barriers to innovation in research practice', in M. Pina, E. Cunha and C. Alves Marques (Eds.), *Readings in Organization Science*, ISDPA, Lisbon, pp. 387–398.

9. Jane Lê and Torsten Schmid, 2022, 'The practice of innovating research methods', *Organizational Research Methods*, 25(2), 308–336, p. 330.

Chapter 5

1. Suzanne Power, 2014, 'Arts-based inquiry: The natural partner for social justice', *The Teacher*, 4 September, www.teachermagazine. com/au_en/articles/arts-based-inquiry-the-natural-partner-for-social-justice, accessed 7/11/2022.
2. Anne Harris, 2018, 'Ethnocinema and video-based research', in P. Leavy (Ed.), *Handbook of Arts-based Research,* Guilford Press, New York, pp. 437–452, p. 439.
3. Jessica Smartt Gullion and Lisa Schäfer, 2018, 'An overview of arts-based research in sociology, anthropology, and psychology', in P. Leavy (Ed.), *Handbook of Arts-based Research,* Guilford Press, New York, pp. 511–525, p. 520.
4. Tristan Tzara, 2022, 'To Make a Dadist [sic] Poem', *The Art History Archive – DADA*, www.arthistoryarchive.com/arthistory/dada/ Tristan-Tzara.html, accessed 7/11/2022.
5. Dawn Mannay, 2010, 'Making the familiar strange: Can visual research methods render the familiar setting more perceptible?', *Qualitative Research*, 10(1), 91–111, p. 100.
6. Ibid., p. 107.
7. Sara Eldén, 2013, 'Inviting the messy: Drawing methods and "children's voices"', *Childhood*, 20(1), 66–81, p. 66.
8. Ibid., p. 72.
9. Jennifer Lapum, Perin Ruttonsha, Kathryn Church, Terrence Yau and Alison Matthews David, 2011, 'Employing the arts in research as an analytical tool and dissemination method', *Qualitative Inquiry*, 18(1), 100–115.
10. Maggie O'Neill, 2008, 'Transnational refugees: The transformative role of art?', *Forum Qualitative Sozialforschung/Forum: Qualitative Social Research*, 9(2), https://www.qualitative-research.net/index. php/fqs/article/view/403, accessed 7/11/2022.
11. Amy Blodgett, Diana A. Coholic, Robert J. Schinke, Kerry R. McGannon, Duke Peltier and Chris Pheasant, 2013, 'Moving beyond words: Exploring the use of an arts-based method in Aboriginal community sport research', *Qualitative Research in Sport, Exercise and Health*, 5(3), 312–331, p. 318.
12. Cited in Paul J. Kuttner, Nick Sousanis and Marcus B. Weaver-Hightower, 2018, 'How to draw comics the scholarly way: Creating comics-based research in the academy', in P. Leavy (Ed.), *Handbook of Arts-based Research,* Guilford Press, New York, p. 406.
13. Helen Kara, 2015, *Creative Research Methods in the Social Sciences: A Practical Guide*, Policy Press, Bristol, p. 6.

14. Cited by Albert Bigelow Paine, 2018, *Mark Twain: A Biography: Volume 2: 1886–1910*, Jazzybee Verlag, Altenmünster, p. 208.
15. Cited by Thomas Dodd, 2019 'Is creativity theft?', Thomas Dodd [blog], 13 June, www.thomasdodd.com/blog/2019/6/13/is-creativity-theft, accessed 7/11/2022.
16. See https://assemblestudio.co.uk/, accessed 7/11/2022.
17. Cited in 'Socially engaged practice', Tate, www.tate.org.uk/art/art-terms/s/socially-engaged-practice, accessed 7/11/2022.
18. Yu Qiping, *Art Markt*, www.artmarkt.net/en/product-category/popular-category/chinese-recorded/yu-qiping/, accessed 7/11/2022.
19. See www.artsy.net/artwork/yu-qiping-yu-qi-ping-lets-talk-about-ordi nary, accessed 7/11/2022; www.artsy.net/artwork/yu-qiping-yu-qi-ping-intoxicated-in-aromatherapy, accessed 7/11/2022.
20. Sarah Kane, 'Blasted', premier 12 January 1995 at the Royal Court Theatre Upstairs, London. See also Sarah Kane, 2001, *Sarah Kane: Complete Plays*, Methuen, London.
21. See www.garciabello.nl/pages/about-us, accessed 7/11/2022.

Chapter 6

1. National Public Radio, 2018, 'Starting your podcast: A guide for students', 15 November, www.npr.org/2018/11/15/662070097/starting-your-podcast-a-guide-for-students, accessed 7/11/2022. Nicole Daniels and Katherine Schulten, 2021, 'Making a podcast that matters: A guide with examples from 23 students', *New York Times*, 26 March, www.nytimes.com/2020/04/22/learning/making-a-podcast-that-matters-a-guide-with-examples-from-23-students.html, accessed 7/11/2022.
2. Marten Scheffer, Matthijs Baas and Tone K. Bjordam, 2017, 'Teaching originality? Common habits behind creative production in science and arts', *Ecology and Society*, 22(2).
3. See Lincoln University, 'Teaching, learning, and student experience', www.lincoln.ac.uk/strategicplan/teachinglearningandstudentexperience/, accessed 7/1//2022.
4. Cited in Travis J. Block et al., 2016, '"Science Fiesta!": Combining student-led community outreach with local culture', *F1000Research*, 5, 2319.
5. Newcastle University, 'Module Catalogue 2022/23: GEO2138: Community Volunteering: A Geography Perspective', www.ncl.ac.uk/module-catalogue/module.php?code=GEO2138, accessed 7/11/2022.
6. Louis Holland Bonnett, North East Childhoods, https://northeast childhoods.org/about-the-project-2/, accessed 7/11/2022.
7. Julia Miao, 2021, 'Adapting medical education initiatives through team-based e-learning, telemedicine objective structured clinical exams, and student-led community outreach during the COVID-19 pandemic', *JMIR Medical Education*, 7(2), e26797.

Staying Original

1. Thomas Carlyle, 1869, *Thomas Carlyle's Collected Works: Volume 6*, Chapman and Hall, London, p14.

Index